Where's the Proof?

True Christianity Verses Religion

Angie Ward

xulon PRESS

Where's the Proof?
True Christianity Verses Religion
by Angie Ward

Printed in the United States of America

ISBN 978-1-60647-065-7

Cover
Cindy Flores, New York City, NY. © 2003.

www.xulonpress.com

4-22-09

To Mike
& Rebecca

Press toward the
goal of the high
calling in Christ Jesus.
It is an honor
serving with you.

love
Angie

You search the
Scriptures,
because you think that
in them you have
eternal life;
and it is these that bear
witness of Me.
                    John 5:39

Jesus answered
and said unto him,
"Truly, truly, I say to
you, unless one is born
again, he cannot see the
kingdom of God."
                    John 3:3

Acknowledgements

I would like to thank my friends, Bill and Ometa Claypole, Steve and Denise Nunley, Barbara Hoffman, and Ginella Calvit for their love, support, and mostly for their prayers. You are all special gifts from God. I thank you.

I also want to thank Pastor Brad Martin and Pastor James Black for reading, correcting, and overall keeping me grounded. Thank you for your wisdom and insight.

I want to thank my husband, Tom, for loving me unconditionally. God used you many times to encourage and push me when I was ready to give up. I am proud that we are partners in this journey. I love you!

Mostly, I want to thank Jesus for calling and choosing me. I have nothing to offer You and You have given me life. Thank you for my salvation! May I finish my race well and bring You glory!

Table of Contents

Introduction... xi
Part 1—The Sower and The Seed.....................19
Part 2—The Soil Analysis..............................31
Part 3—The Problem—The Fall.....................47
Part 4—The Consequences.............................59
Part 5—God's Solution-Blood.......................75
Part 6—The New Covenant............................91
Part 7—What Do You Believe? 117
Part 8—Born Again.....................................135
Part 9—Abraham's Conception and Birth........151
Part 10—Jacob's Conception and Birth...........163
Part 11—Faith Without Works is Dead............175
Part 12—Judas and Hebrews 6 197
Conclusion 227

Introduction

Dear precious reader, I'm not sure why you picked up this book—either the title or the subject matter must have caught your attention. Regardless, I'm glad you did. The goal of this book is to help you, the individual, with the assurance of your salvation. We have the misconception that to question our salvation is a bad thing. Most of the time when people struggle with this, they are immediately told, "It's just the devil trying to tell you that you are not saved. Do not worry about it. I *know* that you are a Christian." Now, I realize that the devil does indeed cause some true believers to doubt their salvation, but I wonder if sometimes it's the Holy Spirit drawing a person to Jesus. Either way, it'll always be to our benefit to examine ourselves to be sure. Paul tells us in 2 Corinthians 13:5-6, *"Test yourselves to see IF you are in the faith; examine yourselves! Or do you not recognize this about yourselves, that Jesus Christ is in you—unless indeed you fail the test?*

But I trust that you will realize that we ourselves do not fail the test."

"Test yourselves." How? Does the Scripture give us a standard that we can measure ourselves by and know for certain the true condition of our souls? I believe so!

Through this book, I would like to extend an invitation to reason the Scriptures together. So, if you do not believe in the infallible and inerrancy of the Scriptures, then you might as well put this book down. Everything I've written is based on the Bible, the very Word of God. Next, we must ask the Holy Spirit for understanding. My prayer is that in this quest you will be willing to lay your heart open and allow God to expose its true condition and discover truths that will transform you and set you free. You see, many people have been taught certain things about God, Jesus, heaven, and hell, and everything in between. Sadly though, most accept them all as truth, never having studied the Word of God for themselves to verify if these things are true or not. Many just blindly believe the doctrines and principles they have been hearing for their entire life. What if they are not true? Are you one of these? Since heaven or hell, life or death, blessings or curses, rest within the Bible, don't you think that *you* should know these truths for yourself? How will you recognize the false doctrines if you do not know the truth?

All of us need to be certain of what we believe. It is also essential to be able to prove them according to the Word of God. In reference to salvation, what have you been taught and what do you believe?

There are teachings that state, "All you have to do is believe certain facts about Jesus and acknowledge Him as your Savior, and you will be saved. It is your profession that confirms your salvation." So many people lead individuals in a sinner's prayer and then tell them, "Now you are saved!" What if that person is *not* truly saved? What if there is more to this believing than we have been taught? Does the Bible speak of *how* to believe? Wouldn't you want to know that little detail?

You and I will stand before God one day and give an account of our stay here on earth. Do you want to be prepared for this appointment? I do, and I'm not willing to take anyone else's word for it!

I'm convinced that every person can search the Bible and examine their heart to see if there is enough evidence to convict them of being a real follower of Jesus Christ. You see, this came as a personal revelation to me. God gave me a glimpse of this truth at a Precept training class about ten years ago. My testimony up to that point was, I went to church and heard about Jesus Christ. I walked an aisle, prayed a prayer, and then I was told that I was saved. I was eight years old at the time. For many years, I read my Bible and tried to go to church. I was not raised in a Christian home, but I believed in God and His Son, Jesus. I was an overall good kid. When I graduated high school and left home, I began a lifestyle that was anything but godly. This lifestyle was a direct contradiction to the Word of God. I went from bad to degrading, but I was convinced that I was a Christian because I believed in Jesus Christ and I had professed Him as my Savior.

For seven years I remained living ungodly until I had used and mistreated so many people that both friends and family had turned their backs on me. I found myself in the depths of sin and alone. I probably hated myself more than anyone else did. One night I cried out to God, as I had *never done before.* I was both real with Him and desperate for Him. I could not go on living like that, *but I did not possess the power to turn my life around.* God met me that night and *truly saved my soul.* At the time, I was twenty-seven, and thought that I had just recommitted my life to Jesus.

I was about forty years old at this Precept training class I mentioned earlier. We were studying Titus and the Scriptures plainly exposed that a real Christian would have good deeds, which I did not possess *before* I had supposedly recommitted my life. God revealed to me that a true follower of Jesus Christ could *not* have a *lifestyle* of sin, that they could not mistreat and use others, and they could not walk away from Jesus like I had done. So seeing the Scriptures and holding my heart up to them both before and after my recommitment, I realized that I was lost all of those years, and if I had died, I most surely would have gone to hell! This, of course, really upset me for I was convinced that I had been a believer since my profession at eight.

From that time, God has continued to show me Scriptures that confirm the fact that a true Christian, a follower of Jesus, will have fruit and proof in their life. Every time I would come across a passage that seemingly contradicted this, I would pray and seek God's wisdom and revelation. He would reaffirm to me this truth. I'm not interested in man's wisdom, I want to know God's truth! Jesus said, *"If you <u>abide in My word, then you are truly disciples of Mine; and <u>you shall know the truth, and the truth shall make you free</u>" (John 8:31-32)*.

The purpose of this book is to disclose what God says about His truly born-again believers and unveil the marks and evidences by which we can *know* if we belong to God or not. In *1 John 3:10* the author writes, *"By this the children of God and the children of the devil are <u>obvious</u>: anyone who does not practice righteousness is not of God, nor the one who does not love his brother."*

By establishing a solid foundation in this matter, my prayer is that you might be able to take hold of these truths and examine yourself, *"to make certain about His calling and choosing you" (2 Peter 1:10)*. In this new light, you can look at your personal experiences at the time of your salvation and evaluate your life against the plumb line of the Scriptures. Whether it was an emotional experience, the sinner's prayer, an altar call, revival meeting, or just a silent cry to God in the solitude of your bedroom, the Scriptures plainly teach that there will be clear indications in your life that you are a child of God. If your life does not line up with the Word of God, I assure you the problem is *not* with God's Word. The error rests with you! You failed the test.

I realize that what I have said so far could be a bit unsettling for you, but please walk together with me and let us see what the Word of God has to say on this subject. You have everything to gain and nothing to lose. The worst thing that can happen by reading this book is that some true Christians might question their salvation. Even this is not a bad thing; remember what Paul admonishes us to do in *2 Corinthians 13:5-6*. When I began studying this truth, I searched for some books on this subject. Unfortunately, there were not many on the market. I did discover one that is priceless. The author is Matthew Mead. He was a Puritan preacher from the 1600's. Mr. Mead wrote a book entitled *The Almost Christian Discovered*. His book addresses this subject wonderfully!

In the writing of his book, Mr. Mead had a concern that it might cause some true Christians to fret and wrestle with the certainty of their salvation. This is also my deep apprehension. In the foreword of *The Almost Christian Discovered*, John MacArthur writes about Mr. Mead's concerns. He states, "Mead realized weak and struggling Christians would read his words and ask, like the innocent disciples in the Upper Room, 'Is it I?'" One of his apparent fears was that some fragile believer might be hurt or discouraged by his indictment. "The Gospel does not speak these things to wound believers," he wrote, "but to awaken sinners and formal professors." He acknowledged the severity of his theme, confessing a certain apprehension. He did not want to "break the bruised reed, nor quench the smoking flax." Yet, his greater fear was that some false Christian might take solace in the promises and comforts of the gospel. Given the choice between consoling a quasi-believer and unsettling someone who is weak in the faith, Mead believed the latter was preferable. He understood the value of self-examination, an exercise modern psycho-evangelicals seem determined to do away with". I have both the same concern and resolve as Mr. Mead.

Lastly, I need to confess that although I believe the things I've written in this book with all my heart, this book is *not* the inspired Word of God. This book is just another commentary on a subject that has been debated for centuries. I acknowledge that I do not have the answers to all the questions that can and will arise from this topic. But I wrote this book with a broken heart for the multitudes of people who I believe have been deceived. I feel compelled with an urgency to get the message out. *"Make sure you are a child of God."*

Matthew 7:21-23 says, ***"Not everyone who says to Me [Jesus], 'Lord, Lord' will enter the kingdom of heaven; but he who DOES the will of My Father who is in heaven. Many will say to Me on that day, 'Lord, Lord, did we not prophesy in Your name, and in Your name cast out demons, and in Your name perform many miracles?' And then I will declare to them, 'I NEVER KNEW YOU; depart from Me, you who practice lawlessness.'"***

He who has ears, let him hear.
Matthew 13:9

The Sower and the Seed
Part One

The reason I wanted to start with this parable is because Jesus lets us know it's the key to understanding all the parables, which also means it's a guide to truth! Look at Mark 4:13, *"And He said to them, 'Do you not understand __this parable__? And __how will you understand all the parables__?"* Jesus is telling His disciples that if they don't get the truths in this parable, they will miss what He is trying to teach in all the rest of them. That tells me there are some important truths here and I don't want to miss them.

I love teaching people how to study the Bible. I hope that after this chapter you'll start examining the Scriptures more carefully. My desire is that the Bible will begin to come alive for you. I must add that the most important step in studying the Bible is prayer! If you are not asking God to show you truth and allow His Holy Spirit to reveal His truth, then you *may not* see it.

Ready? Here we go!

The parable of the sower and the seed is found in three of the gospels—Matthew 13:1-23, Mark 4:1-20, and Luke 8:4-15. Most people will usually just read from one of the gospels, but as you will see, each gospel gives us some insight that the other one does not. Some people say that each gospel comes from three different men's perspective. I agree with that. I also think that God gave each one a piece of a puzzle and unless you read all three you will not have a clear picture of what Jesus is trying to teach us.

As we read the Scriptures, read along with me from your Bible. Get three markers, place them in your Bible by the Scripture references, and turn back and forth with me. This will be a great exercise and you can keep me in check. We will mostly read from Mark, but we will be looking at the other gospels too.

Let's begin with Mark 4:1-9:

And He began to teach again by the sea. And such a very great multitude gathered to Him that He got into a boat in the sea and sat down; and the whole multitude was by the sea on the land. And He was teaching them many things in parables, and was saying to them in His teaching, "Listen to *this! Behold, the sower went out to sow; and it came about that as he was sowing, <u>some seed</u> fell beside the road, and the birds came and ate <u>it</u> up. And <u>other seed</u> fell on the rocky [ground] where <u>it</u> did not have much soil; and immediately <u>it</u> sprang up because <u>it</u> had no depth of soil. And after the sun had risen, <u>it</u> was scorched; and because <u>it</u> had no root, <u>it</u> withered away. And <u>other seed</u> fell among the thorns, and the thorns came up and choked <u>it</u>, and <u>it</u> yielded no crop. And <u>other seeds</u> fell into the good soil and as <u>they</u> grew up and increased, <u>they</u> yielded a crop and produced thirty, sixty, and a hundred-fold." And He was saying, "He who has ears to hear, let him hear."*

The first thing we want to do is determine what the main subject is. This is so essential. By discovering the main subject, we keep everything in its right context. So let's get out your shovel and dig!

After reading Mark, do you think the sower is the main subject? No. Scripture just tells us that he sowed seeds. The sower did not sow differently; he just walked around and tossed seed. Plus, the sower is not mentioned again. Is the subject the soil? No.

Although the Scripture does describe the soil with some detail, it's not the main subject. What about the seed? It appears that the whole parable is all about the seed. Where it fell, the type of soil it landed in, and what happened to it after it fell there. Isn't that just like a farmer? His main objective is that his seed will produce a great harvest.

Now, let's see if the Scriptures will explain to us what the seed *is*. This part is crucial. If we mishandle this, we will misinterpret the whole parable! We will not glean the truths God has for us. So let's proceed carefully.

1) Mark 4:10-14—*"And as soon as He was alone, His followers, along with the twelve, began asking Him about the parables. And He was saying to them, "To you has been given* the mystery of the kingdom of God; *but those who are outside get everything in parables, in order that while seeing, they may see and not perceive; and while hearing, they may hear and not understand lest they return and be forgiven. And He said to them, 'Do you not understand this parable? And how will you understand all the parables? The sower sows the word.'"*

2) Matthew 13:10-19—*And the disciples came and said to Him, "Why do You speak to them in parables?" And He answered and said to them, "To you it has been granted to know* the mysteries of the kingdom of heaven, *but to them it has not been granted. For whoever has, to him shall more be given, and he shall have an abundance; but whoever does not have, even what he has shall be taken away from him. Therefore I speak to them in parables; because while seeing they do not*

see, and while hearing they do not hear, nor do they understand. And in their case the prophecy of Isaiah is being fulfilled, which says, 'You will keep on hearing, but will not understand; and you will keep on seeing, but will not perceive; for the heart of this people has become dull, and with their ears they scarcely hear, and they have closed their eyes lest they should see with their eyes, and hear with their ears, and understand with their heart and return, and I should heal them.' But blessed are your eyes, because they see; and your ears, because they hear. For truly I say to you, that many prophets and righteous men desired to see what you see, and did not see it; and to hear what you hear, and did not hear it. Hear then the parable of the sower. When anyone hears the <u>word of the kingdom</u>, and does not understand it, the evil one comes and snatches away what has been sown in his heart. This is the one on whom seed was sown beside the road."

3) Luke 8:9-12—*And His disciples began questioning Him as to what this parable might be. And He said, "To you it has been granted to* know **the mysteries of the kingdom of God,** *but to the rest it is in parables, in order that seeing they may not see, and hearing they may not understand. Now the parable is this: <u>the seed is the word of God</u>. And those beside the road are those who have heard; then the devil comes and takes away the word from*

their heart, so that they may not believe and be saved."

These Scriptures give us an *indication* of *what the seed* might be:

- The Word (Mark 4:14).
- The Word of the kingdom (Matthew 13:19).
- The Word of God (Luke 8:11).

Now do you know *exactly what the seed is*? Well, yes, it's the Word of God. But what part of the Word of God? All of it? Some of it? Or something very specific? Let's keep looking and see if we can find some more clues. To do this we will continue to look within the context of this parable:

1) Mark 4:12 uses the words, *"lest they return and be forgiven."* The word *return* means to turn around, turn towards, or turn back, a causing of a person to convert. Also in this verse is a phrase, *be forgiven.*
2) Matthew 13:15 says, *"And understand with their heart and return, and I should heal them."* Here it says that an *understanding in their heart* should happen.Then the same word *return* is used. In addition, it talks about *healing them* (Isaiah 6:10).
3) Luke 8:12 makes the strongest statement: *"then the devil comes and takes away the word from their heart, so that they may not*

believe and be saved.'' This verse mentions the expression *"believe and be saved."*

You'll find throughout this book that I make lots of lists. The reason being, many times after we read the Scriptures we forget some things that we read. So by making a list and showing you where the verses are, you are able to *see* what you might have missed! In this list, the Scriptures narrow down the possibility of what the *seed* is:

- Lest they return (be converted) two times,
- and be forgiven,
- understand with their heart,
- I should heal them,
- that they may not believe and be saved.

These words are *synonymous with salvation*, the Good News of God, the gospel. In both the Old and New Testaments, God used these words to warn people of their sinful and hopeless state, and offered an invitation to return to Him. The Old Testament promised a Messiah. In the New Testament, Jesus lets us know, *He is the Messiah*, the Christ! During Old Testament times, men looked ahead to the Messiah in faith. Now men look back to Jesus Christ and the cross. Keep in mind that Jesus is telling this parable, and *it is before His suffering on the cross.* So this is all taking place before any of the New Testament was written. *Before* Paul wrote to us in 1 Corinthians 15:1-4— **"Now I make known to you brethren, the gospel which I preached to you, which also you received,** *in which also you stand, by which also you are saved, if you hold fast the word which I preached to you, unless you believed in vain. For I delivered to you as of first importance what I also received, that Christ died for our sins according to the Scriptures; and that He was buried; and that He was raised on the third day according to the Scriptures."*

Our conclusion: the seed in this parable is the call to man, to turn from his sins, to turn toward God and obtain salvation. It is very important that this is clear to us for if we do not recognize what the seed is, we will not have truth. So, the seed is the gospel! Is there anything else that the words in our word list above could mean? No. In the Old Testament time when this message was preached and man rejected it, salvation did not occur. In the same way as the gospel of Jesus is preached, *if man rejects it there will be no salvation.* I will remind you of this throughout the chapter. As we keep this truth before us, it will help us to *"handle the word of truth accurately"* (*2 Tim. 2:15*).

Now that we have established that the seed is the gospel and *the purpose of the seed being sowed is salvation,* let's see what the seed had in common. We know that all of the seed *fell* on the ground. The same seed that fell on one soil fell on all the soils. It does not say the sower used different seed.

By establishing clearly what each of these symbols represent, we can get a plain understanding of what Jesus is trying to teach us. We must let Scripture speak for itself. Many times people allow their imagination to run wild because they want to add their reasoning to the Word. So it is of utmost importance that we use the Scripture alone for our interpreting it. If the Word is not clear then just leave it alone.

Now we need to find out about the soil. *What is it?* What is its condition? What is the result of the seed sowed in the different soils? Was anything produced because of the gospel sowed? These are significant questions that we need to answer! Now let's go back to the parable for the rest of the story.

1) Mark 4:13-15—*"And He said to them, 'Do you not understand this parable? And how will you understand all the parables? The sower sows the word. And these are the ones who are beside the road where the word is sown; and when they hear, immediately Satan comes and takes away the <u>word which has been sown IN THEM</u>.'"*

2) Matthew 13:18-19—*"Hear then the parable of the sower. 'When anyone hears the word of the kingdom, and does not understand it, the evil one comes and snatches away <u>what has been sown IN HIS HEART</u>.'"*

3) Luke 8:12, 15—*"And those beside the road are those who have heard; then the devil comes and takes away <u>the word from THEIR HEART</u>, so that they may not believe and be saved. And the seed in the good soil, these are the ones who have heard the <u>word in an honest and good HEART</u>, and hold it fast, and bear fruit with perseverance."*

Here is our list concerning what the soil is:

- the word which has been sown in them (Mark 4:15)
- what has been sown in his heart (Matt. 13:19)
- the word from their heart (Luke 8:12)
- the word in an honest and good heart (Luke 8:15).

So you see what the Scriptures say? *The soil is the heart!* These people heard the Word, the gospel, and it was sown in their hearts, all of them. We see in Matthew 13:19 that the devil came and took away the Word *from* their heart. Teaching this parable I have had people say, "If the Word is *in* man's heart, how can the devil come and take it?" Well, I do not know, but this is what the Scriptures tell us, so I believe it's so!

Now let us review what we have learned so far:

1) The sower sowed the seed.
2) The seed is the main subject in this parable, how it was sown, where it fell, and what happened to this seed after it fell.
3) The seed was all sown the same.
4) The seed sown is the gospel.
5) The seed was sown into men's hearts.
6) The purpose of sowing the seed, the gospel, was so that man may believe and be saved.

Amazing! I don't know about you, but when I first saw these truths, I was surprised. It is very exciting to see clearly what the Bible says for yourself. No commentaries, just the Bible. Now, don't get me wrong, these do have their place, but we have become lazy and want other people to tell us truth when God has placed His Word in our hands. We can *see* it for ourselves and we should!

Compared to what you have been taught about this parable, have you *seen* anything different? Did you notice that Scripture revealed its own interpretation? We do not need to figure out Scripture, we just need to let the Holy Spirit unveil its truth. In the following section we'll be examining each soil and making some lists. I believe you are in store for some wonderful truths that you will *see* for yourself.

For the gate is small,
and the way is narrow
that leads to life,
and few are those who find it.
Matthew 7:14

The Soil Analyses
Part Two

My son Jay used to work at a business that both sold and installed pools. When he would do maintenance on the pools, he would take a tester to verify the PH of the water. He used this information to calculate the chlorine needed for suitable swimming. Likewise, our local 4-H office takes soil samples and runs tests on them to see the composition of the different soils. We are going do to the same thing. We will take the Word of God, examine it, and see exactly what it says. We will make some lists and compare all four soil samples together. I'm convinced that the results will be quite a surprise for most of you. Let's get digging!

SOIL # 1 Beside the Road

1) Mark 4:15—*And these are the ones who are beside the road where the word is sown; and when they hear, immediately Satan comes and takes away the word which has been sown in them.*
2) Matthew 13:19—*When anyone hears the word of the kingdom, and does not understand it, the evil one comes and snatches away what has been sown in his heart. This is the one on whom seed was sown beside the road.*
3) Luke 8:12—*And those beside the road are those who have heard; then the devil comes and takes away the word from their heart, so that they may not believe and be saved.*

SOIL #1 Beside the Road

1) They heard the Word (Mk. 4:15; Matt. 13:19; Luke 8:12).
2) They did not understand the word (Matt. 13:19).
3) The evil one (Satan) came and immediately takes away the word which was sown in their hearts (; Mk. 4:15; Matt. 13:19: Luke 8:12).
4) So that they may not believe and be saved (Luke 8:12).

This could be anyone. They hear the gospel and it is sowed in their heart but, *they do not understand it.* The devil then comes and takes the word immediately from their heart and they are not saved. The purpose of the gospel was *not* obtained in this person. Seed was sowed but immediately it was taken; nothing occurred, nothing was produced. No salvation!

SOIL #2 Rocky Places

1) Mark 4:16-17—*And in a similar way these are the ones on whom seed was sown on the rocky places, who, when they hear the word,* **immediately** *receive it with joy; and they have no firm root in themselves, but are only temporary; then, when affliction or persecution arises because of the word,* **immediately** *they fall away.*

2) Matthew 13:20-21—*And the one on whom seed was sown on the rocky places, this is the man who hears the word, and* **immediately** *receives it with joy; yet he has no firm root in himself, but is only temporary, and when affliction or persecution arises because of the word,* **immediately** *he falls away.*

3) Luke 8:13—*And those on the rocky soil are those who, when they hear, receive the word with joy; and these have no firm root; they believe for a while, and in time of temptation fall away.*

SOIL #2 Rocky Places

1) They hear the Word (Mk. 4:16; Matt.13:20; Luke 8:13).
2) Immediately received it with joy (Mk. 4:16; Matt. 13:20; Luke 8:13).
3) These have no root in themselves (Mk. 4:17; Matt. 13:21; Luke 8:13).
4) They are temporary (Mk. 4:17; Matt. 13:21).
5) When afflictions or persecutions arise because of the Word, immediately they fall away (Mk. 4:17; Matt. 13:21).
6) They believed for awhile, and in time of temptation fell away (Luke 8:13).

In this soil, we see a little more occurring. These people heard the Word, and they immediately *received it* with joy. Let's take a look at the word *received*. A few translations use the word *received* in both Mark 4:16 (Soil #2) and Mark 4:20 (Soil #4). The NASB uses the word *accept* for Soil #4 (v. 20) and correctly so. In the original Greek text these are two different words. Here in Soil #2 (the rocky places), the word for *received* means to take or receive. Many times it suggests a self-prompted taking. In Mark 4:20, Soil #4 (the good soil), the word for *received* means to receive with agreement.

It is apparent from the definitions that the word used in verse 16 can very well be a person who sees something that could benefit them, so they take it. As we continue to look at Soil #2, we will see if that makes sense. Remember, at this point we want to know *what the condition of the soil is and what happened to the seed after it fell.* As we chug away, we must remember that the soil is man's heart and the seed is the gospel. An invitation for man to turn toward God; *if* they accept Him they will be saved.

The words or phrases used in connection with Soil #2 are:

1) Immediately—We saw that as fast as they *received it* (the gospel), they *"immediately fell away."* Why? Persecution arose because of the gospel. (Mk. 4:17; Matt. 13:21).

2) Mark 4:17—*"They have no root in themselves."* They *do not have a firm hold* on the gospel in their life. The gospel had been preached, and it was received with joy, but they had *"no root in them,"* and so they plainly rejected the gospel when it came time to *prove* (persecution) *that they truly believed* in God.

3) Mark 4:17 and Matthew 13:21 say they are *"but temporary."* This word temporary means, *for the occasion only.*

4) Luke 8:13 says, *"they believed for a while."* Salvation does not occur with this shallow type of faith.

5) Luke 8:13—*"in time of temptation [they] fall away."* Let's see what these words mean. Temptation: it means a putting to proof. Fall away: it means to revolt or desert.

John 6:66 says, **"As a result of this many of His disciples withdrew, and were not walking with Him anymore."** In this context of John, Jesus just finished speaking some hard words, and these disciples grumbled at what He said. Then they went back and walked with Him *no more!* They never followed Jesus again. Sound familiar? It appears that the people in Soil #2 did the same thing. They turned back from following God!

Actually, there does not seem to be anything in these verses that might lead us to believe that salvation had taken place. They had believed for awhile, but when they were put to the test, they rejected the very gospel that could have saved them! Here, as in Soil #1, *nothing* had been produced as a result of the gospel preached! It appears that there was some change in their lives, but because they just believed for awhile, the change was not permanent. The result was that they went back to how they were before. Second Peter 2:20: **"For if after they have escaped the defilements of the world by the knowledge of the Lord and Savior Jesus Christ, they are again entangled in them and are overcome, the last state has become worse for them than the first."**

Let's see if the verses at the beginning of the parable confirm what we have found:

1) Mark 4:5-6—**"And other seed fell on the rocky ground where it did not have much soil; and <u>immediately it sprang up</u> because it had no depth of soil. And after the sun had**

> risen, it was scorched; and because it had no
> root, it <u>withered away</u>."

2) Matthew 13:5-6—"*And others fell upon the rocky places, where they did not have much soil; and <u>immediately they sprang up</u>, because they had no depth of soil. But when the sun had risen, they were scorched; and because they had no root, they <u>withered away</u>.*"

3) Luke 8:6—"*And other seed fell on rocky soil, and as soon as <u>it grew up, it withered away</u>, because it had <u>no moisture</u>.*"

In Mark and Matthew we saw that the seed immediately sprang up; there was some growth, but "when the sun had risen," affliction and persecutions because of the gospel, it, the seed, was scorched and it (the gospel), withered away. Now for any of you who are plant lovers, if your plant is scorched by the sun and dries up, what hope is there for the plant? None! Keep in mind that this is not what was done to the person, but to the gospel that was preached. The gospel was scorched and dried up.

The words *grew up* in Luke 8:6 mean *to bring forth, produce*. There appeared to be some life but it was a temporary thing. Why? Because there was no depth of soil, and no root in them. The gospel that was preached to them did not produce salvation, yet there appeared to be change.

Let's look at Soil #3:

SOIL #3 Among the Thorns

1a) Mark 4:7—*"And other [seed] fell among the thorns, and the thorns came up and choked it, and it yielded no crop."*

1b) Mark 4:18-19—*"And others are the ones on whom seed was sown among the thorns; these are the ones who have heard the word, and the worries of the world, and the deceitfulness of riches, and the desires for other things enter in and choke the word, and it becomes unfruitful."*

2a) Matt. 13:7—*"And others fell among the thorns, and the thorns came up and choked them out."*

2b) Matt. 13:22—*"And the one on whom seed was sown among the thorns, this is the man who hears the word, and the worry of the world, and the deceitfulness of riches choke the word, and it becomes unfruitful."*

3a) Luke 8:7—*"And other seed fell among the thorns; and the thorns grew up with it, and choked it out."*

3b) Luke 8:14—*"And the seed which fell among the thorns, these are the ones who have heard, and as they go on their way they are choked with worries and riches and pleasures of this life, and bring no fruit to maturity."*

As you can see for the third soil, I'm using both the parable and Jesus' interpretation *together*. I felt like you could see some things more clearly this way. Many students of the Bible say that this third soil is a Christian, a backslidden Christian, who has no fruit in his life. This soil will reveal most, the importance of discovering *exactly* what the *seed* is, the gospel. Well, let's see what the Word of God does say!

Here is our list:

SOIL #3 Among the Thorns

1) They heard the word (Mk. 4:18; Matt. 13:22; Luke 8:14).
2) The Word sown (fell) among the thorns (Mk. 4:18; Matt. 13:22; Luke 8:14).
3) The worries of the world and the deceitfulness of riches (and the desires for other things entered in) choked the word, the gospel (Mk. 4:19; Matt. 13:22).
4) They are choked with worries, riches, and the pleasures of this life (Luke 8:14).
5) (It) the word (the gospel) became unfruitful (Mk. 4:19; Matt. 13:22).
6) They bring no fruit to maturity (Luke 8:14).

Since this seed (the gospel) fell among the thorns, I want to allow the Scriptures to establish what these thorns are. Three of the gospels tell us that they are: *"and the worries of the world, and the deceitfulness of riches, and the desires for other things."*

Let's look more closely at this phrase:

39

1) Worries—to draw in different directions, to distract.
2) Deceitfulness—that which gives a false impression.
3) Desires—a craving, a longing, mostly for evil desires.
4) Pleasures—the natural desires or sinful desires.

All these words are pointing to *this world*, this life, the here and now. In these Scriptures none of them says "worries of this world OR deceitfulness of riches" etc. But they say *and* the worries of this world *and* the deceitfulness of riches *and* the desires for other things, not *or*. It is the combination of all of these, *"And the worries of the world, and the deceitfulness of riches, and the desires for other things."* Not some or one of them but *all of them*. These people have heard the gospel and go on their way. They want it all. All of what God has to offer and the world. In the end they settle for what the world has. It does not sound like they have responded to the invitation to repent and turn to God. This is just one clue; let's keep looking.

In both Mark and Matthew it states these thorns *choke the word* (the gospel) and it (*the gospel*) *becomes unfruitful*. The word *choked* means to strangle completely, to drown, or to crowd out. The word *unfruitful* means barren. Now understand the verses in Mark and Matthew: they say that the gospel was choked and produced nothing.

Remember the purpose of the gospel sown in a person's heart is to bring salvation. This did not happen. The gospel and its saving power was choked, crowded out of these people's hearts because of the cares of the world.

Luke 8:14—*"And the seed which fell among the thorns, these are the ones who have heard, and as they go on their way they are choked with worries and riches and pleasures of this life, and bring no fruit to maturity."* Here it talks about the result to the *individual*; it's the same outcome as the gospel. They were choked and brought no fruit to maturity. This makes perfect sense; if the gospel is unfruitful in a person's life, if they do not become a believer, then it only makes sense that the person will also bring no fruit to *maturity*.

Our conclusion: this person had some sort of fruit similar to Soil #2. The gospel appeared to have produced life, but in the end, the gospel preached proved to be fruitless. The soil (the heart), where the gospel was sown among the thorns, it showed more life than Soil #2. They went on their way, but at last somewhere in the journey they forsook the gospel for the world. The gospel held no meaning or worth to them, so they sold the truth for the riches of the world.

Now I'm hearing some of you saying, "She believes you can lose your salvation." No! No! No! I'm not saying that at all. In fact according to the Scriptures, *I most surely do believe in eternal salvation!* What I am saying, is that somewhere *between* the gospel being preached to these people, and them choosing to accept it, to repent, turn to God, and allow Him to heal them, they went back and forsook God. They did not accept God's plan for fallen man. They were *never* saved. Yes, they might have walked an aisle and prayed the sinner's prayer and even believed all the facts about Jesus but that is not what produces salvation.

How long can the journey be between the gospel preached, and a person choosing to accept or reject God? I don't know. For some it could be years. Many people make a profession, and join a church. They might be there, doing all the religious duties for twenty years or more, and then just fall away, never to walk with God and Jesus again. If that is the case, more than likely they were *never saved* to start with. Church attendance is not the proof that you are a Christian! What is your measuring stick? Have you had a great experience and that is your proof? Have you made a profession that you believe in Christ? Do you go to church, read your Bible, or do you pray? Well, a person can do all of these things and still be lost and on their way to hell.

Now look at our last soil:

Soil #4 The Good Soil

1) Mark 4:20—*"And those are the ones on whom seed was sown on the good soil; and they <u>hear the word</u> and <u>accept it</u>, and <u>bear fruit</u>, thirty, sixty, and a hundredfold."*

2) Matt. 13:23— *"And the one on whom seed was sown on the good soil, this is <u>the man</u>*

> *who hears the word and understands it; who*
> *indeed bears fruit, and brings forth, some a*
> *hundredfold, some sixty, and some thirty."*

3) Luke 8:15—*"And the seed in the good soil,*
these are the ones who have heard the word
in an honest and good heart, and hold it fast,
and bear fruit with perseverance."

Here's our list:

Soil # 4 The Good Soil

1) An honest and good heart (Luke 8:15).
2) Hears the word (Mk. 4:20; Matt. 13:23; Luke 8:15).
3) Understands the word (Matt. 8:23).
4) Accepts it (Mk. 4:20).
5) Holds (it) the word fast (Luke 8:15).
6) Bears fruit, some 100, 60, 30, with perseverance (Mk. 4:20; Matt. 13:23; Luke 8:15).

In this soil, the Bible describes to us the condition of the heart; it is honest and good (Luke 8:15). The other soils were not good. They had no depth, they were rocky, or there were thorns growing in them. If our hearts are not right, the gospel will not produce salvation.

Here we are told that this is the man who hears the word (the gospel) and understands it, the gospel, whereby men are saved (Matthew 13:23). Remember Soil #1? He did not understand the gospel, so Satan was able to snatch it from his heart.

In Soil #4 the Bible also tells us that they accept it, the gospel (Mark 4:20). Remember in Soil #2, we talked about this word accept? It means to receive or admit with approval. We agree with God about who He is, and who we are. We are lost sinners in need of a savior. We agree and believe that if we repent and turn to God, He will heal us, forgive us, and save us from our sins.

We are also told in these passages that this good soil are the ones who hold it (the gospel) fast (Luke 8:15). The phrase *hold it fast* means to hold firmly to. They held firmly to the gospel. They saw its value and did not give it up when trials came. Whereas Soil #2, the rocky soil, was only temporary and when persecution arose because of the *word* (the gospel) they immediately turned loose of *the word* and fell away.

Soil #4 is the only one that bore fruit: ***"who indeed bears fruit, and bring forth, some a hundredfold, some sixty, and some thirty" (Matt. 13:23).*** The difference between them was the amount of fruit they produced, some a hundredfold, some sixty, some thirty, but they *all did produce fruit*, none of the other soil did. Plus, soil #4 they bore fruit with perseverance. The word *perseverance* means cheerful, hopeful, enduring, or constant. These people *continued in the faith*, nothing detoured them. That means all the way through their lives, that they endured to the end. Not like that of Soil #3, "among the thorns" they went their way for a while but they failed to *continue*.

Our conclusion to the parable of the sower and the seed is that *only* Soil #4, the last soil, the good soil, the one with a good heart, who responded with an honest heart to the gospel, was truly a believer, a true Christian. He had everything the others lacked, he understood *it* (the gospel), accepted *it*, he bore fruit, held fast *the word* (the gospel), and persevered. These are *some of the marks of a Christian*. There are more; we will cover them in this book.

Within this parable lies the proof that Christians *will* have fruit in their lives, proving that they are a child of God. The result of the gospel preached to the first three soils produced nothing. We saw that in each case *the seed* (the gospel) was prevented from bearing fruit, the bringing forth of salvation in a person's soul. Because of this, they did not have the ability to continue, and their faith was in vain!

> *"Now I make known to you, brethren, the gospel which I preached to you, which also you received, in which also you stand, by which also you are saved, IF you hold fast the word which I preached to you, unless you believed in vain."*

1 Corinthians 15:1-2

What about you? Is there fruit in your life, proving that you are a Christian? Are you just hopeful, crossing your fingers that you're a child of God's? Have you believed in vain? I hope not!

Look at the chart below, soil #4 had everything that the other soils were missing.

A COMPARISON CHART
FOR THE SOILS FOUND IN THE SOWER
AND THE SEED

SOIL # 1 Beside the Road

1) They heard The Word *(Mk 4:15)*
   (Matt. 13:19) (Luke 8:12)
2) They did not understand The Word
   (Matt 13:19)
3) The evil one (satan) (devil) came and
   immediately takes away The Word
   which was sown in their hearts (in
   them) *(Mk 4:15) (Matt 13:19) (Luke
   8:12)*
4) So that they may not believe and be
   saved *(Luke 8:12)*

SOIL # 2 Rocky Places

1) They hear The Word
   (Mk 4:16) (Matt 13:20 (Luke 8:13)
2) Immediately received it with joy
   (Mk 4:16) (Matt 13:20) (Luke 8:13)
3) These have no root in themselves *(Mk 4:17)*
   (Matt 13:21) (Luke 8:13)
4) They are temporary *(Mk 4:17) (Matt 13:21)*
5) When afflictions or persecutions arise
   because of The Word, immediately they fall
   away *(Mk 4:17) (Matt 13:21)*
6) They believed for awhile, and in time of
   temptation fall away *(Luke 8:13)*

SOIL # 3 Among the Thorns

1) They heard the Word *(Mk 4:18) (Matt 13:2)*
   (Luke 8:14)
2) The Word sown (fell) among the thorns
   (Mk 4:18) (Matt 13:22) (Luke 8:14)
3) The worries of the world and the deceitfulness
   of riches (and the desires for other things
   entered in) choked the Word (The Gospel)
   (Mk 4:19) (Matt 13:22)
4) They are choked with worries, riches &
   pleasures of this life *(Luke 8:14)*
5) (It) The Word (The Gospel) became
   unfruitful *(Mk 4:19) (Matt 13:22*
6) They bring no fruit to maturity *(Luke 8:14)*

Soil # 4 The Good Soil

1) An honest and good heart
   (Luke 8:15)
2) Hears the Word *(Mk 4:20)*
   (Matt 13:23) (Luke 8:15)
3) Understands the Word
   (Matt 8:23)
4) Accepts it *(Mk 4:20)*
5) Holds (It) the Word fast
   (Luke 8:15)
6) Bears fruit, some 100, 60, 30
   (With perseverance) *(Mk 4:20)*
   (Matt 13:23) (Luke 8:15)

*For they [man] exchanged
the truth of God for a lie,
and worshipped and served
the creature
rather than the Creator,
who is blessed forever.
Amen.*
                    Romans 1:25

The Problem—the Fall
Part Three

A s I undertake the task before me, I would like
to reflect on the words of Matthew Mead. His
book, *The Almost Christian Discovered*, is very
sobering and is certainly not for feel good reading.
I believe we have too many of those kinds of books
and not enough that would challenge readers to ask
themselves the most important question: "Am I
truly a child of God?" This is what Mr. Mead said

to his readers, "You have here one of the saddest considerations imaginable presented to you, and that is how far it is possible a man may go in a profession of religion and yet, after all, fall short of salvation; how far he may run and yet not so run as to obtain. This, I say, is sad, but not so sad as true; for our Lord Christ plainly attests it: 'Strive to enter in at the strait gate: for many, I say unto you, will seek to enter in, *and shall not be able.*"

My desire for you, the reader, is that you will give me the privilege of reasoning the Scriptures with you, and to help you understand what God's Word says on the subject of proof in the life of believers.

First, I feel we must go back to the beginning and try to see how man fell and found himself in need of salvation.

In the beginning, God created the heavens and the earth. Then God said, "Let us make man in our image, according to our like-ness; and let them rule over the fish of the sea and over the birds of the sky and over the cattle and over all the earth, and over every creeping thing that creeps on the earth." Then the Lord God formed man of dust from the ground, and breathed into his nostrils the breath of life; and man became a living being. And the Lord God planted a garden toward the east, in Eden; and there He placed the man whom He had formed (Genesis 1:1, 26; 2:7-8).

Man was alive both physically and spiritually. God had created man and desired fellowship with him. Here man found himself in an ideal atmosphere; the conditions were at their best for perfect unity with the God of the universe. Man knew his Creator. God's presence was with man, and God walked with man. All that man ever needed was found in God. *Stop!* Now I want us to look at two verses. Genesis 2:16-17 says, *"And the Lord God commanded the man [Adam], saying, "From any tree of the garden you may eat freely; but from the tree of the knowledge of good and evil you shall not eat, for in the day that you eat from it, you shall surely die."* It's interesting to note that in Genesis 2:9, God said first, *"And out of the ground the Lord God caused to grow every tree that is pleasing to the sight and good for food; the tree of life also in the mist of the garden, AND the tree of the knowledge of good and evil."* Therefore, both trees were there, both pleasing to the sight and both good for food. Here we find God giving Adam *one* commandment, just one, mind you. God basically said, "You can have any and every tree in the garden for food, just look around and pick. They are all great, they all taste wonderful, and all will satisfy your hunger but you *cannot* eat of the tree of knowledge of good and evil!"

On the surface, it appears that Adam wanted what was forbidden. The only thing God said he could not have, he desired. Nevertheless, I wonder if that was really the problem. Was it about desiring something forbidden or was the root another issue? Why did God do this? Why did He put that tree there if He did not want Adam to eat from it? Why didn't God leave everything out that might disrupt His fellowship with Adam? Was it an option between trees, or was Adam put to the test? I'm convinced that God was testing Adam to see if he would trust Him. If Adam could trust God, then he would also obey Him, thus making his Creator his Lord and Master.

Let us go to the third chapter of Genesis to witness the events. Genesis 3:1-5 —

> *Now the serpent was more crafty than any beast of the field which the Lord God had made. And he said to the woman, "Indeed, has God said, 'You shall not eat from any tree of the garden?'" And the woman said to the serpent, "From the fruit of the trees of the garden we may eat; but from the fruit of the tree <u>which is in the middle of the garden</u>, God has said, 'You shall not eat from it or touch it, lest you die.'" And the serpent said to the woman, "You surely <u>shall not die</u>! For God knows that in the day you eat from it your eyes will be opened, <u>and you will be like God, knowing good and evil</u>."*

As the story unfolds, we encounter the serpent. How does the Bible describe him? Crafty: *"more crafty than any beast of the field."* We also see that he came to Eve, the woman, the weaker vessel (1 Peter 3:7). Yes, I know that this is not politically correct but I do not think God cares. According to Genesis 3:3, Eve said, *"But from the fruit of the tree which is __in the MIDDLE of the garden__, God has said, 'You shall not eat from it or touch it, lest you die.'"* I do not think that Eve and the serpent were standing in front of the tree of knowledge during this conversation. If they were, Eve would not have made reference to it being in the middle of the garden. Rather, she would have said something like, *"But from the fruit of THIS tree, God has said, 'You shall not eat from it or touch it, lest you die.'"* Also, Adam is not mentioned; it is very likely that he was not there during this discourse. This is an interesting point, because remember, God gave this command to Adam not to his wife Eve.

The serpent tries to confuse Eve. He says, *"Indeed, has God said you shall __not eat__ from __any__ tree of the garden?"* She then corrects him, *"From the fruit of the trees of the garden we may eat; but from the fruit of the tree which is in the middle of the garden, God has said 'You shall not eat from it __or touch it lest you die__.'"* In this verse, we have Eve adding to God's command. He did not say *if you touch it* you will die but *"for in the day that you __eat__ from it you shall surely die!"*

Upon further consideration, we notice the serpent's real objectives. One: he tempts *Eve to doubt God's word, to question His character.* Maybe God really did not mean, *"You shall surely die,"* as if God could lie! Two: he entices *Eve to question God's love for her.* Could He be trusted? Did God, their Creator, really have their best interests in mind? Would God give them every good and perfect thing they needed? Notice how the serpent shrewdly tosses out, *"For God knows that in the day that you eat from it your eyes will be opened, and <u>you will be like God</u>, knowing good and evil" (Gen. 3:5).* We can almost hear Eve's thoughts, "Surely we could use this wisdom. Why would God hold this back from us?" The serpent causes Eve to take her eyes off God and begin looking at herself to meet her own needs, and ultimately becoming her own god!

This last phrase, *you will be like God*, is what caused Satan, the serpent, to rebel against God in the first place. Satan wanted to be like God. Read with me in Isaiah 14:12-14: *"How you have fallen from heaven, O star of the morning, son of the dawn! You have been cut down to the earth, You who have weakened the nations! But you said in your heart, <u>I will ascend to heaven; I will raise my throne above the stars of God, and I will sit on the mount of assembly</u> in the recesses of the north. <u>I will ascend above the heights of the clouds; I will make myself like the Most High.</u>"*

Hear what Satan said in his heart:

- I will ascend into heaven.
- I will raise my throne above the stars of God.
- I will sit upon the mount of assembly, in the recesses of the north.
- I will ascend above the heights of the clouds.
- I will make myself like the Most High.

Keep in mind that Satan was a created being. He knew God; he was one of God's powerful angels. But Satan did not want to acknowledge God or worship

Him. He wanted to be exalted and worshiped. He did not want anyone else telling him what to do. He wanted to be like God, the one in control. So Satan was tempting Eve the same way. Satan caused her to doubt God and not trust Him. Maybe she started thinking, "Why should I bow and serve God when I could be like God? Maybe I need to take control of my own life. Maybe God doesn't really love me or care what's best for me."

So let's see if Satan's plan worked. Let's look at Genesis 3:6-7: *"When the <u>woman saw that the tree was good for food</u>, and that it was <u>a delight to the eyes</u>, and that <u>the tree was desirable to make one wise, she took from its fruit and ate; and</u> she gave also to <u>her husband with her, and he ate</u>. Then the eyes of both of them were opened, and they knew that they were naked; and they sewed fig leaves together and made themselves loin coverings."*

Here we now have Adam and Eve standing by the tree. There are three things that appealed to Eve; it was good for food, a delight to the eyes, and was desirable to make one wise. First John 2:15-17 also speaks about these three desires—*"Do not love the world, nor the things in the world. If anyone loves the world, the love of the Father is not in him. For all that is in the world, <u>the lust of the flesh, and the lust of the eyes, and the boastful pride of life</u>, is not from the Father, but is from the world. And the world is passing away, and also its lust; <u>but the one who does the will of God abides for ever.</u>"* Eve was more concerned with satisfying her desires than obeying God. She was consumed with lust and therefore deceived. It is interesting to note what the Bible says about the events in Genesis 3:6-7: *"For it was Adam who was first created, and then Eve. And it was not <u>Adam who was deceived</u>, but <u>the woman being quite deceived</u>, fell into transgression" (1 Timothy 2:13-14).* Eve was the one deceived; yet Adam committed sin because he disobeyed God and ate the fruit Eve gave him. They both listened and yielded to someone other than God.

In conclusion, we find that Adam and Eve did not trust God; consequently, they disobeyed Him. That first couple made the decision to serve themselves, not God.

The result of their decision caused all of humanity to be separated from God. The fellowship that man once enjoyed with his Creator had ceased. Speaking on this subject, the apostle Paul writes in his letter to the church at Rome:

For the wrath of God is revealed from heaven against all ungodliness and unrighteousness of men, who suppress the truth in unrighteousness, because that which is known about God is evident within them; for God made it evident to them. For since the creation of the world His invisible attributes, His eternal power and divine nature, have been clearly seen, being understood through what has been made, so that they are without excuse. For even though they knew God, they did not honor Him as God, or give thanks; but they became futile in their speculations, and their foolish heart was darkened. Professing to be wise, they became fools, and exchanged the glory of the incorruptible God for an image in the form of corruptible man and of birds and four-footed animals and crawling creatures. Therefore God gave them over in the lusts of their hearts to impurity, that their bodies might be dishonored among them. For they exchanged the truth of God for a lie, and worshiped and served the creature rather than the Creator, who is blessed forever. Amen (Romans 1:18-25).

Let's make a list:

- That which is known about God *is evident within them*; for *God made it evident to them.*
- for since the creation of the world His invisible attributes, His eternal power and divine nature, *have been clearly seen, being understood* through what has been made, *so that they are without excuse.*
- For even though they knew God, they did not honor Him as God, or give thanks. *They exchanged the truth of God for a lie, and <u>worshiped and served the creature rather than the Creator.</u>*

You see man would rather worship and serve the creature than the Creator. Consequently, when Adam and Eve failed to obey God, they revealed their lack of trust in Him. By their disobedience, they exposed this heartbreaking fact, that man would rather worship and serve the creature than the Creator, thus making themselves to be God!

I would like to bring one more thing to your attention. I want to remind you that there were two trees, the tree of life and the tree of knowledge of good and evil. When man was given the choice of life or death, he chose death. We do not find that Adam or his wife ever ate of the tree of life. See Genesis 3:22, 24—*"Then the Lord God said, 'Behold, the man has become like one of us, knowing good and evil; and now, lest he stretch out his hand, and take also from the tree of life, and eat and live forever.' So He drove the man out; and at the east of the garden of Eden He stationed the cherubim, and the flaming sword which turned every direction, to guard the way to the tree of life."*

It's a similar choice Moses gave the children of Israel right before they were to go into the Promised Land. Deuteronomy 30:15-20—

See, I have set before you today life and prosperity, and death and adversity; in that I command you today to love the Lord your God, to walk in His ways, and to keep His commandments and His statutes and His judgments, that you may live and multiply, and that the Lord your God may bless you in the land where you are entering to possess it. But if your heart turns away and you will not obey, but are drawn away and worship

other gods and serve them, I declare to you today that you shall surely perish. You shall not prolong your days in the land where you are crossing the Jordan to enter and possess it. I call heaven and earth to witness against you today, that I have set before you life and death, the blessings and the curse. So choose life in order that you may live, you and your descendants. By loving the Lord your God, by obeying His voice, and by holding fast to Him; for this is your life and the length of your days, that you may live in the land which the Lord swore to your fathers, to Abraham, Isaac, and Jacob, to give them.

Does this sounds familiar? Obey God and live. Disobey God and you perish!

*For the wages of sin
is death
but the free gift of God is
eternal life
in Christ Jesus our Lord.*
                    Romans 6:23

The Consequences
Part Four

T he definition of consequence is the natural result of an action. God had said to Adam in Genesis 2:16-17, *"And the Lord God commanded the man, saying, 'From any tree of the garden you may eat freely; but from the tree of the knowledge of good and evil you shall not eat, for in the day that you eat from it, you shall surely <u>die</u>.'"* The penalty for Adam's disobedience was death. Remember, at the beginning Adam was alive both physically and spiritually. *"Then the Lord God formed man of the* *dust from the ground, and breathed into his nostrils the breath of life; and man became a <u>living being</u>" (Genesis 2:7).* God warned Adam, *"For in the day that you eat from it you shall surely die!"* Yet we find in Genesis 5:5, *"So all the days that Adam lived were <u>nine hundred and thirty years, and he died.</u>"* Adam and Eve did not die physically that day, they *died spiritually.* The result of rejecting God by disobeying Him (sin) brought the *penalty of death.*

James 1:13-16 says, *"Let no one say when he is tempted, 'I am being tempted by God'; for God cannot be tempted by evil, and He Himself does not tempt anyone. But each one is tempted when he is carried away and enticed by <u>his own lust.</u> Then when <u>lust has conceived,</u> it gives <u>birth to sin;</u> and when <u>sin is accomplished,</u> it brings forth <u>death.</u> Do not be deceived, my beloved brethren."* This is what happened to Eve in Genesis 3:6, *"When the woman saw that the tree was good for food, and that it was a delight to the eyes, and that the tree was desirable to make one wise, she took from its fruit and ate; and she gave also to her husband with her, and he ate."* Eve had been carried away and enticed by her own lust. When her lust conceived, it gave birth to sin, and sin always brings forth death. God said that sin (disobedience) would bring death and it did. Adam listened to his wife instead of the voice of God; so on that day, they died.

Romans 5:12-21 reveals that this death was passed down to all of mankind.

*Therefore, just as through <u>one man sin</u>
<u>entered into the world</u>, and <u>death through</u>
<u>sin, and so death spread to all men, because</u>
<u>all sinned</u> for until the Law sin was in the
world; but sin is not imputed when there is no
law. Nevertheless death reigned from Adam
until Moses, even over those who had not
sinned in the likeness of the offense of Adam,
who is a type of Him who was to come. But
the free gift is not like the transgression. For
if <u>by the transgression of the one the many</u>
<u>died</u>, much more did the grace of God and
the gift by the grace of the one Man, Jesus
Christ, abound to the many. And the gift is
not like that which came through the one
who sinned; for on the one hand the judgment arose from one transgression resulting
in <u>condemnation</u>, but on the other hand the
free gift arose from many transgressions
resulting in justification. For if by the transgression of the one, <u>death</u> reigned through
the one, much more those who receive the
abundance of grace and of the gift of righteousness will reign in life through the One,
Jesus Christ. So then as through one transgression there resulted <u>condemnation to all</u>
<u>men</u>, even so through one act of righteous-
ness there resulted justification of life to all
men. For as through the one man's <u>disobe-
dience</u> the <u>many were made sinners</u>, even so
through the obedience of the One the many
will be made righteous. And the Law came*

> ***in that the transgression might increase; but where sin increased, grace abounded all the more, that, <u>as sin reigned in death</u>, even so grace might reign through righteousness to eternal life through Jesus Christ our Lord.***

Because of Adam's sin all mankind suffers the penalty:

- Through one man sin entered into the world (verse 12)
- and death through sin (verse 12)
- and *so death spread to all men, because all sinned* (verse 12).
- By the transgression of the one the many died (verse 15)
- and judgment arose from one transgression resulting in condemnation (verse 16)
- for if by the transgression of the one, death reigned through the one (verse 17)
- so then as through one transgression there resulted *condemnation* to all men (verse 18). Basically, condemnation means the sentence has been pronounced and we are damned to hell.
- Through the one man's disobedience, the many were made sinners (verse 19).
- Sin reigned in death (verse 21).

Adam's sin brought death, judgment, and condemnation to all mankind. Mankind was *in* Adam, so when Adam sinned, *all* mankind sinned too (Rom. 5:12).

Now this statement, that mankind was *in* Adam, might be hard to understand so let me clarify by giving an illustration. Your great grandfather, like all men, had the seeds or sperm for reproduction *in* him. The future generations of your family were *in* him, including you. Now if your great grandfather died before he married and had children, neither your grandfather, your father, nor you would have ever been born. So the same principle is true with Adam. Before he had any children, the human race was *in* him and when he sinned all men sinned also.

Adam's penalty became our penalty. When God said, *"In the day you eat from it you shall surely die,"* all mankind died with Adam a spiritual death. When we are born, we are born sinners. Before anyone accepts Jesus Christ as Savior and Lord, we are dead men walking. We are dead spiritually, lost, and without hope until God reveals His precious Son to us.

In Romans 3, Paul explains man's lost condition,

What then? Are we better than they? Not at all; for we have already charged that both Jews and Greeks are <u>all under sin</u>; as it is written, there is <u>none righteous</u>, not even one; there is <u>none who understands</u>, there is <u>none who seeks for God;</u> all have turned aside, together they have become <u>useless</u>; there is none who does good, there is not *even one. Their throat is an open grave, with their tongues they keep deceiving, the poison of asps is under their lips; whose mouth is full of cursing and bitterness; their feet are swift to shed blood, <u>destruction</u> and <u>misery</u> are in their paths, and the path of peace have they not known. There is <u>no fear of God</u> before their eyes,<u> for all have sinned and fall short of the glory of God</u> (Romans 3:9-18, 23).*

Let's see what this lists looks like:

- all under sin
- none righteous, not even one
- none who understands
- none who seeks for God
- all have turned aside
- they have become useless
- none who does good
- not even one
- their throat is an open grave
- with their tongues they keep deceiving
- the poison of asps is under their lips
- whose mouth is full of cursing & bitterness
- destruction & misery are in their paths
- their feet are swift to shed blood
- the path of peace have they not known
- there is no fear of God before their eyes

For all have sinned and fall short of the glory of God!

Do you see man's hopeless state? There is not one person, man, woman, or child who comes close to God's holiness. No matter how good you are, or someone you may know, no matter how wonderful *we appear* on the outside, we are all evil and *all* fall short!

Genesis 3:6-11 gives us some additional consequences to Adam's refusal to trust and obey God.

When the woman saw that the tree was good for food, and that it was a delight to the eyes, and that the tree was desirable to make one wise, she took from its fruit and ate; and she gave also to her husband with her, and he ate. Then the eyes of both of them were opened, and they knew that they were naked; and they sewed fig leaves together and made themselves loin coverings. And they heard the sound of the Lord God walking in the garden in the cool of the day, and the man and his wife hid themselves from the presence of the Lord God among the trees of the garden. Then the Lord God called to the man, and said to him, "Where are you?" And he said, "I heard the sound of Thee in the garden, and I was <u>afraid</u> because I was <u>naked</u>; so I <u>hid</u> myself." And He said, "Who told you that you were naked? Have you *eaten from the tree of which I commanded you not to eat?"*

For the first time we see that man is self-conscious: *"They knew that they were naked."* They *hid* themselves from the presence of God because they were *afraid*. Here we have more consequences because of disobedience: *guilt*, *shame* and *fear*. These were emotions that neither Adam nor his wife had ever experienced before. At this point, we find them *hiding* from God. Sin always brings a separation between man and God. Man pulls away from God because of his guilt and God separates Himself because He is holy and man has become unholy. Due to this, the fellowship that man once had with God has been broken!

Finally, we see that Adam and his wife's failure to obey God brought curses upon them and the serpent. Let us look at them. Genesis 3:14-15: *"And the Lord God said to the serpent, "Because you have done this, cursed are you more than all cattle, and more than every beast of the field; on your belly shall you go, and dust shall you eat all the days of your life; and I will put enmity between you and the woman, and between your seed and her seed; <u>He shall bruise you on the head</u>, and you shall bruise him on the heel."* It appears, according to verse fourteen, that the serpent had walked uprightly in the beginning. God pronounced that it would now crawl on its belly, *"All the days of your life."* The other half of the curse is verse fifteen. I want us to look at this very closely. God said, *"And I will put <u>enmity</u>*

___between you and the woman___, *and between your seed and her seed."* The word *enmity* means to be an enemy of someone, to be hostile towards, to hate. The women represented the remnant of God's people down through the ages, which would be birthed into God's kingdom. The serpent is the devil himself; he hates God, Jesus, and His people. God says that there would always be this hostility between the two. Turn to Revelation 12:17: *"And the dragon was enraged with the woman, and went off to make war with the rest of her offspring, who keep the commandments of God and hold to the testimony of Jesus."*

This hatred would also be between the serpent's seed and the women's seed. *"And I will put enmity between you and the woman, and between ___your seed and her seed___; He shall bruise you on the head, and you shall bruise him on the heel."* The word for *seed* here is singular, meaning one, not many. This is confirmed in the next phrase. When it is said that, *"He* shall bruise you on the head" it speaks of a specific person. This person is Jesus Christ, God's only Son, sent to destroy the works of the devil.

In 1 John 3:8 it says, *"The one who practices sin is of the devil; for the devil has sinned from the beginning. The Son of God appeared for this purpose, that He might destroy the works of the devil."* Genesis 3:15 is one of the most awesome Scriptures in the Bible, for it is in this small verse that God first promises man a Savior, Jesus *"the Lamb of God who takes away the sin of the world!"* John 1:29. He would defeat the devil and restore fellowship between God and man.

From the beginning, we find God's mercy in the midst of His judgment. Even before God pronounced the curses on man, He had a solution, *Jesus*, to man's greatest problem, *sin*. Man had found himself lost, without hope, and separated from his Creator and yet God already had a plan to bring him back.

Although God gave man hope, there were still consequences to man's sin. Genesis 3:16-19:

> *To the woman He said, "I will greatly multiply your <u>pain</u> in childbirth, in pain you shall bring forth children; yet your desire shall be for your husband, and he shall rule over you." Then to Adam He said, "Because you have listened to the voice of your wife, and have eaten from the tree about which I commanded you, saying, 'You shall not eat from it'; <u>cursed is the ground</u> because of you; <u>in toil you shall eat of it</u> all the days of your life. <u>Both thorns and thistles it shall grow for you</u>; and you shall eat the plants of the field; <u>by the sweat of your face you shall eat bread</u>, till you return to the ground, because from it you were taken; for you are dust, and to dust you shall return."*

Look at these curses:

A. *I will greatly multiply your <u>pain</u> in child-birth, in pain you shall bring forth chil-dren* (verse 16). Here God is telling Eve that her pain and sorrow would increase greatly as she goes into labor and her children are birthed. Yet, there is more. He also says that in the raising of children there will be much pain and toil as she tries to bring them up. Remember, because of Eve's rebellion all mankind became sinners. So likewise her children would also be rebellious. Of course, not all to the same degree.

This can be seen with all small children. We do not have to teach them to be selfish or mean. But we do have to teach them to share and be nice. Some professionals would have us believe that mean, selfish kids come from mean environments. Not so! They come from Adam and are all selfish and need to be taught not to bite or take toys from each other and to be nice. If you have raised children, you know this is true.

As Eve and all moms try to raise their children, there is much pain and sorrow that comes. Again, not all suffer the same. Some children are easier to raise. But I believe all would agree that motherhood is not easy and that is because of man's sin nature.

B. *Yet your <u>desire</u> shall be for your husband, and he shall <u>rule</u> over you"* (verse 16).

As we keep in mind that the context of this statement is sin and judgment, we must also remember that Eve called the shots at the forbidden tree. I think it's very possible that what God could be saying is this, "You will want to run the show but I'm putting Adam in charge over you." Since this was a curse, we can assume that Adam and Eve were equal before God. No one was in charge or ruling over the other; but now that had changed.

I would like to add a note here. Ephesians 5:22 says, *"Wives, be subject to your own husbands, as to the Lord."* Now I know that there are many men who take this out of context. It does not mean that wives are to be a doormat. Nor is God giving him the right to mistreat and abuse their wives. Those who do abuse this God-given authority never read or work out the rest of those passages. Ephesians 5:25: *"Husbands, love your wives just as Christ also loved the church and gave Himself up for her."* But women, as God commands us, we must try not to rule over our husbands.

Now back to the consequences and the curses:

C. ***Cursed is the ground** because of you* (verse 17).

D. ***In toil you shall eat of it** all the days of your life* (verse 17).

E. ***Both thorns and thistles it shall grow for you; and you shall eat the plants of the field* (verse 18).

F. ***By the sweat of your face you shall eat bread, till you return to the ground* (verse 19).

It appears that before the fall there were no weeds, thorns, or thistles. It was with ease that Adam worked in the garden. Now the ground was cursed and Adam was going to have to work very hard for it to produce the food needed to sustain him and his family.

If you've ever worked in a garden you know that the *only* thing that grows easy are the weeds. I don't know where they come from but you can just about watch them grow. The weeds will overtake a garden quickly and choke out the produce that you are trying to grow. So it takes a lot of continual hard work to have a successful garden.

Adam and Eve's actions, brought pain and suffering upon themselves and all mankind. The first couple never would have experienced these, *if* they would have trusted God and obeyed His command. This fact has not changed; there is always a price to pay when we disobey God. Please understand this, when you and I disobey God, He will always forgive us when we come with true humility and repent of our sins but there will always be consequences for our disobedience. Some of these will follow us the rest of our lives.

Let's summarize the lists of consequences that were passed down to you and me and all mankind because of Adam and Eve's disobedience:

- through one man sin entered into the world
- and death through sin
- and so death spread to all men, because all sinned
- by the transgression of the one the many died

- judgment arose from one transgression resulting in condemnation
- for if by the transgression of the one, death reigned through the one
- so then as through one transgression there resulted condemnation to all men
- through the one man's disobedience the many were made sinners
- sin reigned in death
- all under sin
- their throat is an open grave
- none righteous, not even one
- with their tongues they keep deceiving
- none who understands
- the poison of asps is under their lips
- none who seeks for God
- whose mouth is full of cursing and bitterness
- all have turned aside
- their feet are swift to shed blood
- they have become useless
- destruction and misery are in their paths
- none who does good
- the path of peace have they not known
- not even one
- there is no fear of God before their eyes
- *for all have sinned and fall short of the glory of God!*
- guilt, shame, and fear
- I will greatly multiply your pain in childbirth, in pain you shall bring forth children
- yet your desire shall be for your husband, and he shall rule over you.

- cursed is the ground because of you
- in toil you shall eat of it all the days of your life
- both thorns and thistles it shall grow for you; and you shall eat the plants
- by the sweat of your face you shall eat bread, till you return to the ground

Is there hope for mankind? Yes there is! Things look hopeless, but God has a plan. His mercy endures forever!

For the life of the flesh is in the blood,
and I have given it to you on the altar to make atonement
for your souls:
for it is the blood by reason of the life
that makes atonement.
Leviticus 17:11

God's Solution-Blood
Part Five

God gave man an avenue where he could once again approach Him and have the fellowship that was lost by man's fall. His solution was blood! Although Jesus would not appear for 4,000 years, God points to Him by the sacrifice of animals. We find this first in Genesis 3:20-21—*"Now the man*

called his wife's name Eve, because she was the mother of all the living. And <u>the Lord God made garments of skin</u> for Adam and his wife, and clothed them." This verse is very significant; because this is the first time that any blood had been shed. God had all the animals, along with man, eat only plants. Genesis 1:29-30—*Then God said, "Behold, I have given you every plant yielding seed that is on the surface of all the earth, and every tree which has fruit yielding seed; it shall be food for you; and to every beast of the earth and to every bird of the sky and to every thing that moves on the earth which has life, I have given every green plant for food; and it was so."* Up to this time, animals did not kill or eat each other. However, here it is said that, *"<u>The Lord God made garments of skin</u> for Adam and his wife, and clothed them."*

I believe here God took an animal and sacrificed it for man's benefit. The skins were used to clothe them physically, but the blood that was shed, God used to cover their sins.

From before time God had a plan that the blood of His Son Jesus would pay the price to redeem man from his lost state. Revelation 13:8: *"And all who dwell on the earth will worship him [the Beast], everyone whose name has NOT been written <u>from the foundation of the world</u> in the book of life of <u>the Lamb who has been slain</u>."* John 1:29 shows us God's Lamb and His purpose: *"The next day he saw Jesus coming to him, and said, 'Behold, the Lamb of God <u>who takes away the sin of the world!</u>'"*

Through the sacrifice of that first animal, God laid down the requirement for sin, **blood**. Although the Scriptures do not speak of a conversation between God and Adam explaining the blood covering man's sin, we do see from the beginning that Abel (Genesis 4:4), and Noah (Genesis 8:20-21), understood what type of offering God would accept. So I believe God had to have communicated this with Adam. How else did they know? Guess? I don't think so.

Turn with me to Genesis 4:1-7—

Now the man had relations with his wife Eve, and she conceived, and gave birth to Cain, and she said, "I have gotten a manchild with the help of the LORD." And again she gave birth to his brother Abel. And Abel was a keeper of flocks, but Cain was a tiller of the ground. So it came about in the course of time that Cain brought an offering to the LORD of the fruit of the ground. And Abel, on his part also brought of the firstlings of his flock and of their fat portions. And the LORD had regard for Abel and for his offering; but for Cain and for his offering He had no regard. So Cain became very angry and his countenance fell. Then the LORD said to Cain, "Why are you angry? And why has your countenance fallen? If you do well, will not your countenance be lifted up? And if you do not do well, sin is crouching at the door; and its desire is for you, but you must master it."

Verse 4 and 5 say God had respect for Abel and his offering but not for Cain and his offering. God would not have accepted one offering and rejected another if He had not made it clear what He expected. Abel brought the blood sacrifice, but Cain ignored God's way of making an offering (the blood) and brought to Him fruit of the ground. Cain was trying to come to God his own way, and we can see God was not pleased with him.

Countless people say, "There are many ways to God." But Jesus told us, *"I am the way, and the truth, and the life; no one comes to the Father, but through Me" (John 14:6).* According to Jesus, there is only one way to God and it is through the precious blood of Jesus Christ. Yes this might be narrow-minded and intolerable to some people, but nevertheless, it is the truth.

Leviticus 17:1-6 reveals how man had been carrying out the sacrifices for sin from Adam until the time God brought up the children of Israel out of Egypt and gave them the law; 17:1-6—

Then the Lord spoke to Moses, saying, Speak to Aaron and to his sons, and to all the sons of Israel, and say to them, This is what the Lord has commanded, saying, <u>Any man from the house of Israel who slaughters an ox, or a lamb, or a goat in the camp, or who slaughters it outside the camp, and has not brought it to the doorway of the tent of meeting to present it as an offering to the Lord before the tabernacle of the Lord,</u>

bloodguiltiness is to be reckoned to that man.
He has shed blood and that man shall be cut
off from among his people. The reason is so
that the sons of Israel may bring their sacri-
fices which they were sacrificing in the open
field, that they may bring them in to the
Lord, at the doorway of the tent of meeting
to the priest, and sacrifice them as sacrifices
of peace offerings to the Lord. And the priest
shall sprinkle the blood on the altar of the
Lord at the doorway of the tent of meeting,
and offer up the fat in smoke as a soothing
aroma to the Lord.

This law was given to the children of Israel because God now wanted man to begin bringing sacrifices to Him *in a particular way.* Before that, man had set up their altars in open fields and brought their sacrifices to God.

The next Scripture tells us more about the blood; Leviticus 17:10-12— *"And any man from the house of Israel, or from the aliens who sojourn among them, who eats any blood, I will set My face against that person who eats blood, and will cut him off from among his people. For the life of the flesh is in the blood, and I have given it to you on the altar to make atonement for your souls; for it is the blood by reason of the life that makes atonement. I said to the sons of Israel, 'No person among you may eat blood, nor may any alien who sojourns among you eat blood.'"*

What the blood accomplishes:

- For the life of the flesh is in the blood
- I have given it to you on the altar to make atonement for your souls
- it's the blood by reason of the life that makes atonement

Adam, because of his sin, brought death to himself and all mankind. Since the life of the flesh is in the blood, God requires that a death take place to restore life.

Andrew Murray, in his book, *The Blood of Christ* says:

When we think of bloodshed, we think of death; death follows when the blood or the soul is poured out. Death makes us think of sin, for death is the punishment for sin. God gave Israel the blood on the altar as the atonement or covering for sin; that means the sins of the transgressor were laid upon the victim, and its death was reckoned as the death or punishment for the sins laid on it.

Blood, therefore, signifies the life given up to death for the satisfaction of the law of God and in obedience to His command. Sin was so entirely covered and atoned for, it was no longer reckoned as that of the transgressor. He was forgiven.

The book of Hebrews talks extensively about Jesus being the believer's high priest. It covers the New Covenant in relationship to the Old Covenant. Hebrews reveals how the blood was the main instrument in both covenants, what the two have in common, and what is different. Turn to Hebrews 9:1-7 —

Now even the <u>first covenant had regulations of divine worship</u> and the earthly sanctuary. <u>For there was a tabernacle prepared, the outer one</u>, in which were the lampstand and the table and the sacred bread; this is called the holy place. And <u>behind the second veil</u>, there was a tabernacle which is called the Holy of Holies, having a golden altar of incense and the ark of the covenant covered on all sides with gold, in which was a golden jar holding the manna, and Aaron's rod which budded, and the tables of the covenant. And above it were the cherubim of glory overshadowing the mercy seat; but of these things we cannot now speak in detail. Now when these things have been thus prepared, the priests are continually entering the outer tabernacle, performing the divine worship, <u>but into the second only the high priest enters, once a year, not without taking blood, which he offers for himself and for the sins of the people committed in ignorance</u>.

The Old Covenant

- The Old Covenant had regulations of divine worship (v. 1).
- The tabernacle had two rooms, the outer one called the holy place, where the priests are continually entering the outer tabernacle, performing the divine worship (vss. 1-2, 6).
- The second room was called the Holy of Holies. Into this part, only the high priest entered once a year, *not without [taking] blood*, which he offers for himself and for the sins of the people committed in ignorance (vss. 3, 7).

This yearly event mentioned is called the Day of Atonement. The regulations were given in Leviticus 16. Notice the main item for entering the Holy of Holies was the blood.

>*<u>But when Christ appeared as a high priest of the good things to come, He entered through the greater and more perfect tabernacle</u>, not made with hands, that is to say, not of this creation; and <u>not through the blood of goats and calves, but through His own blood</u>, He entered the holy place once for all, having obtained eternal redemption. For <u>if the blood of goats and bulls and the ashes of a heifer sprinkling those who have been defiled, sanctify for the cleansing of the flesh, how much more will the blood of Christ, who through the eternal Spirit</u>*

offered Himself without blemish to God, cleanse your conscience from dead works to serve the living God? And for this reason He is the mediator of a new covenant, in order that since a death has taken place for the redemption of the transgressions that were committed under the first covenant, those who have been called may receive the promise of the eternal inheritance (Hebrews 9:11-15).

The New Covenant

- Christ appeared as high priest and entered heaven with His own blood (vs. 11-12).
- In the Old Covenant, the blood of animals was used for the sanctifying of the flesh (vs. 12-13).
- Notice the *much more* effect of the blood of Christ. Jesus, who through the eternal Spirit, *offered Himself without blemish to God, cleanses your conscience from dead works to serve the living God.* (vs. 14)

Through His blood, Jesus has obtained eternal redemption. The word for *redemption* means to buy back, or purchase something. For example, when someone is kidnapped, the criminals send a ransom note asking for money. In order for them to release the person held captive, the payment must be made. Because of Adam's refusal to trust and obey God, he sold himself to his enemy, and mankind has been held ransom by the devil ever since.

A payment was needed to rescue mankind. A transaction needed to take place. Therefore, Jesus offered Himself without blemish to God and brought His blood. Notice, the blood was given to God. He was the One who needed to be satisfied. Isaiah 53:10-12 says—

> *But the Lord was pleased to crush Him, putting Him to grief; if He would render Himself as a guilt offering, He will see His offspring, He will prolong His days, and the good pleasure of the Lord will prosper in His hand. As a result of the anguish of His soul, He will see it and be SATISFIED; by His knowledge the Righteous One, My Servant, will justify the many, as He will bear their iniquities. Therefore, I will allot Him a portion with the great, and He will divide the booty with the strong; because He poured out Himself to death, and was numbered with the transgressors; yet He Himself bore the sin of many, and interceded for the transgressors."*

Jesus became man's substitute. He paid the price for mankind and God was satisfied. Now, whenever man accepts Jesus as his Savior and Lord, His blood is applied to them and God forever sees *the blood* and they are accepted. Their sins are forgiven and they are justified before God. They are no longer condemned, lost, spiritually dead.

Psalm 103:12 says, *"As far as the east is from the west, so far has He removed our transgressions from us."* How awesome is this! That God would clean us up and so remove *all* our sins, to be clean! No more guilt or shame; totally forgiven. If that doesn't make you want to shout, maybe you've never experienced it.

And if you address as Father, the One who impartially judges according to each man's work, conduct yourselves in fear during the time of your stay upon earth; knowing that <u>you were not redeemed with perishable things</u> like silver or gold from your futile way of life inherited from your forefathers, <u>but with precious blood, as of a lamb unblemished and spotless, the blood of Christ</u>. For He was foreknown before the foundation of the world, but has appeared in these last times for the sake of you who through Him are believers in God, who raised Him from the dead and gave Him glory, so that your faith and hope are in God, (1 Peter 1:17-21).

Have you been purchased by the blood of Jesus Christ? God has declared that a sacrifice was needed; blood had to be shed for forgiveness in order for man to be brought back to God. Have you accepted God's sacrifice for your sins? If not, there does not remain any other hope for you. Jesus spoke these words in John 8:24: *"I said therefore to you, that you shall die in your sins; for unless you believe that I am He, you shall die in your sins."*

Do you see how Adam's sin brought death, but Jesus, *"through one act of righteousness there resulted justification of life to all men."*

Let's compare Adam to Jesus: Romans 5:1-21

In Adam

- Through one man sin entered into the world (v. 12)
- and death through sin (v. 12)
- and so death spread to all men, because all sinned (v. 12).
- By the transgression of the one the many died (v. 15)
- judgment arose from one transgression resulting in condemnation (v. 16).
- For if by the transgression of the one, death reigned through the one (v. 17)
- so then as through one transgression there resulted condemnation to all men (v. 18)
- through the one man's disobedience the many were made sinners (v. 19)
- sin reigned in death (v. 21).

In Christ Jesus

- We have **peace** with God through our Lord Jesus Christ (v. 1)

- whom also we have had our access by faith into this grace wherein we stand (v. 2)
- we **rejoice in hope** of the glory of God (v. 2)
- we also **rejoice in our tribulations** (v. 3)
- the **love of God hath been shed abroad in our hearts through the Holy Spirit which was given unto us** (v. 5).
- **Christ died for the ungodly** (v. 6).
- **While we were yet sinners** Christ died for us (v. 8).
- Much more then, being now **justified by his blood,** shall we be **saved from the wrath [of God]** (v. 9).
- **While we were enemies,** we were **reconciled to God through the death of His Son** (v. 10);
- much more, being reconciled, shall **we be saved by his life** (v. 10).
- We also rejoice in God through our Lord Jesus Christ, through whom we have now received the reconciliation (v. 11).
- The free gift is not like the transgression (v. 15)
- much more did the grace of God and the gift by the grace of the one man, Jesus Christ, abound to the many (v. 15).
- And the gift is not like that which came through the one who sinned (v. 16)
- the free gift arose from many transgressions **resulting in justification** (v. 16)
- much more those who receive **the abundance of grace** and of **the gift of righteousness will**

reign in life through the One, **Jesus Christ** (v. 17)
- through one act of righteousness there resulted **justification of life** to all men (v. 18)
- through the obedience of the **One the many will be made righteous** (v. 19)
- **so grace might reign through righteousness to eternal life** through **Jesus Christ our Lord** (v. 21).

Although Adam's one act of disobedience (sin) brought death and condemnation to the whole human race, Jesus' one act of obedience made all those who trust in Him righteous and right before a holy God. His one act canceled the debt that man could not pay. Someone once told me a little story to help me understand judgment, mercy, and grace. It goes like this. One day a man was driving on the interstate and he was speeding because he was late for an appointment. He heard the sirens first; then looked in the mirror. A sickening feeling came over him as he saw the police car right behind him. He pulled over and got his paperwork together as the policeman approached his car.

There are two likely possibilities that can happen next:

1. **Judgment**—The policeman could give him a ticket because he was speeding and broke the law. He would have a large fine and it would go against his record.

2. **Mercy**—The policeman could just give him a warning. He still deserves a ticket, but mercy would have been shown.

But what would happen if the policeman wrote the ticket against himself instead of the man speeding, paid the fine, and had the points go against his record? What if he let the man go free? That would be *grace*, and that is what Jesus Christ did for us. He died for mankind so no one would have to die and spend an eternity in hell separated from God. He paid the price for our sins and made a way for us to have fellowship with God once more. His mercy endures forever!

We sing a song in our churches. The name of it is, *There Is Power in the Blood.* I declare to you that there is truly power in the blood of Jesus Christ. His blood covers man's sin and justifies him before a holy God. It also gives us entrance into the New Covenant. In Matthew 26:26-28 we hear Jesus' words: ***"And while they were eating, Jesus took some bread, and after a blessing, He broke it and gave it to the disciples, and said, 'Take, eat; this is My body.' And when He had taken a cup and given thanks, He gave it to them, saying, 'Drink from it, all of you; for this is My blood of the covenant, which is poured out for many for forgiveness of sins.'"*** In the New Covenant (which we will see in the next chapter) God *enables* man to live godly in an ungodly world. If I believed anything otherwise, I would find me another god. If God cannot do a work in me in this life, can I really trust that He can bring me to heaven after death! NO!

*The secret of the Lord is for
those who fear him,
and He will make them
know His covenant.*
Psalm 25:14

The New Covenant
Part Six

In this chapter we will discover the richness of the New Covenant. It is the very reason that there will be proof in a believer's life that they are truly one of God's children. Within this New Covenant, God makes us promises, and these promises come to all believers at the time of their salvation. The believers do not begin to possess these promises *after* they are taught to them. They are facts that happen to a believer at the *very moment* they are born again, without knowing these truths, without them being taught, without even understanding them. As God supernaturally births us into His kingdom, He equips us for that kingdom. Yes, some of the promises of God must be worked out in faith, but the promises found in the New Covenant, God Himself says, "I will," and He does.

Examine with me, the New Covenant. Jeremiah 31:31-34—

"Behold, days are coming," declares the Lord, "when I WILL make a <u>new covenant</u> with the house of Israel and with the house of Judah, <u>not like the covenant which I made with their fathers</u> in the day I took them by the hand to bring them out of the land of Egypt, My covenant which they broke, although I was a husband to them," declares the Lord. "But this is the covenant which I WILL make with the house of Israel after those days," declares the Lord, "I WILL <u>put My law within them, and on their heart I WILL write it</u>; and I WILL be their God, and they shall be My people. And they shall not teach again, each man his neighbor and each man his brother, saying, 'Know the Lord,' for they shall all know Me, from the least of them to the greatest of them," declares the Lord, <u>"for I WILL forgive their iniquity, and their sin I WILL remember no more."</u>

When will God make a New Covenant and with *who*?

- *Days are coming*—this is something that was to happen in the future (v. 31).
- *God will make a new covenant with the house of Israel and the house of Judah* (v. 31).

Now before we can go any further, we must establish *who* exactly this New Covenant is to. Some believe that this is only to the Jewish believers, and not to the Gentile believers. Others say that this Scripture is for the thousand-year reign and not for the church now.

Let's see what the Scriptures reveal to us:

1) Ephesians 2:11-22—

Therefore remember, that formerly you, the Gentiles in the flesh, who are called "Uncircumcision" by the so-called "Circumcision," which is performed in the flesh by human hands remember that you were at that time separate from Christ, excluded from the commonwealth of Israel, and STRANGERS TO THE COVENANTS OF PROMISE, having no hope and without God in the world. BUT NOW IN CHRIST JESUS YOU WHO FORMERLY WERE FAR OFF HAVE BEEN BROUGHT NEAR BY THE BLOOD OF CHRIST. For He Himself is our peace, who made both groups into one, and broke down the barrier of the dividing wall, by abolishing in His flesh the enmity, which is the Law of commandments *contained in ordinances, that in Himself <u>He might make the two into one new man,</u> thus establishing peace, and might reconcile them <u>both in one body</u> to God through the cross, by it having put to death the enmity. And He came and preached peace to you who were far away, and peace to those who were near; for through Him we <u>both have our access in one Spirit to the Father.</u> So then you are no longer strangers and aliens, but you are fellow citizens with the saints, and are of God's household, having been built upon the foundation of the apostles and prophets, Christ Jesus Himself being the corner stone, in whom the whole building, being fitted together is growing into a holy temple in the Lord; in whom you also are being built together into a dwelling of God in the Spirit.*

Let us make our list:

A) Paul is talking to *"<u>the Gentiles in the flesh,</u> who are called "Uncircumcision" by the so-called "Circumcision"* (v. 11).

B) *"Remember that you were at that time <u>separate</u> from Christ, <u>excluded</u> from the commonwealth of Israel, and <u>strangers</u> to the covenants of promise, having <u>no hope and without God in the world</u>"* (v. 12).

Before salvation, the gentile believers were:

1. separated from Christ (v. 12),
2. excluded from the commonwealth of Israel (v. 12),
3. strangers to the *covenants of promise* (v. 12),
4. having no hope (v. 12),
5. without God in the world (v. 12).

C) ***"BUT now in Christ Jesus you who formerly were far off have been brought near by the blood of Christ*** (v. 3).

Now, in Christ Jesus, they (the Gentile believers) are no longer separated, excluded, or strangers.

1. They were far off, but now have been brought near by the blood of Christ (v. 13).
2. Christ is our peace (v. 14).
3. Christ has made both groups (Jews and Gentiles) into one (v. 14).
4. Christ broke down the barrier of the dividing wall (v. 14).
5. Christ did this by abolishing in His flesh the enmity (a reason for opposition) which is the Law of commandments contained in ordinances (v. 15).
6. That Christ might make the two into one new man, establishing peace (v. 15).
7. That Christ might reconcile them both in one body to God through the cross (v. 16).

8. Christ came and preached peace to both groups (v. 17).
9. Through Christ, we both have our access in one Spirit to the Father (v. 18).
10. ***"So then you are no longer strangers and aliens, but you are fellow citizens with the saints, and are of God's household"*** (v. 19).

According to these Scriptures, God has made the two—Jews and Gentiles—into one man, *in* Christ Jesus. Do you see that the Gentile believers are now *included* in the commonwealth of Israel; they are no longer *strangers to the covenants of promise* but now what was promised to the Jews are our promises also. They are fellow citizens with the saints, and are of God's household.

2) John 10:15-16—*"Even as the Father knows Me and I know the Father; and I lay down My life for the sheep. And I have other sheep, which are not of this fold; I must bring them also, and they shall hear My voice; and they shall become one flock with one shepherd."*

A) Christ has other sheep.
B) They are not of this fold (meaning not Jewish).
C) They shall hear His voice.
D) Both folds shall be ONE flock.
E) They will have one shepherd.

3) Galatians 3:25-29— *"But now that faith has come, we are no longer under a tutor. For you are all sons of God through faith in Christ Jesus. For all of you who were baptized into Christ have clothed yourselves with Christ. <u>There is neither Jew nor Greek</u>, there is neither slave nor free man, there is neither male nor female; for you are <u>all one in Christ Jesus</u>. And if you belong to Christ, then you are Abraham's offspring, heirs according to promise."*

  A) You are all sons of God through faith in Christ Jesus.
  B There is not Jew or Greek (Gentile).
  C) For you are all one in Christ Jesus.
  D) And if you belong to Christ then you are Abraham's offspring, *heirs according to promise.*

4) Romans 9:1-8—

I am telling the truth in Christ, I am not lying, my conscience bearing me witness in the Holy Spirit, that I have great sorrow and unceasing grief in my heart. For I could wish that I myself were accursed, separated from Christ for the sake of my brethren, my kinsmen according to the flesh, who are Israelites, to whom belongs the adoption as sons and the glory AND THE COVENANTS and the giving of the Law *and the temple service and the promises, whose are the fathers, and from whom is the Christ according to the flesh, who is over all, God blessed forever. Amen. But it is not as though the word of God has failed. <u>For they are not all Israel who are descended from Israel; neither are they all children because they are Abraham's descendants, but: "through Isaac your descendants will be named." That is, it is not the children of the flesh who are children of God, but the children of the promise are regarded as descendants</u>.*

Again, who is Israel?

- For they are not all Israel who are [descended] from Israel (v. 6).
- Neither are they all children because they are Abraham's descendants (v. 7).
- Through Isaac your descendants will be named (v. 7).
- It is not the children of the flesh who are children of God (v. 8).
- But the children of the promise are regarded as descendants (v. 8); those who have accepted Jesus as Savior.

Not all of the Jewish people who are the descendants of Abraham are the children of God because, *"<u>it is not the children of the flesh who are children of God, but the children of the promise are regarded</u>*

as descendants." Remember Galatians 3:29: *"And if you belong to Christ, then you are Abraham's offspring, heirs according to promise."*

Therefore, as Gentile believers, *everything* that God promised to the Jewish believers in the New Covenant belongs to us. Even the land. The believer's land is the same one Abraham went out in search of—Hebrews 13:9-10, 13-16. The Jewish people will have the physical land of Israel. Yes, I realize that God still has a plan for the nation of Israel, but the promises in the New Covenant are for all believers *in* Christ. Romans 1:16 says, *"For I am not ashamed of the gospel: for it is the power of God for salvation to everyone who believes; to the Jew first, and also to the Greek."*

Well, now that we have established who the New Covenant is for, we can begin studying it and discover what God promised to those who believe and accept His Son, Jesus Christ. You must realize that everything that God did in the past, everything He does now, and all that He will do, is based on covenant. What we cover in this section is by no means an exhaustive study on the subject. Volumes have been written about covenant. There are many areas of covenant that will not be discussed in this book. What we will cover here are the promises God makes when we enter the New Covenant with Him.

My goal is to help you see clearly *why*, as truly born-again believers, men will have proof that they are genuine, one of God's own children. Down through the ages there have always been false professors in the church. People claiming to be God's children, but are not. The enemy has always tried to sneak into the church, disguise himself as one of God's own, and malign the truth. Yet, I also believe that there are those who have been deceived; they truly believe they are saved but are not. These truths are for the church. We must examine God's Word and ourselves.

Let's go back to Jeremiah 31:31-34—

"<u>Behold, days are coming," declares the Lord</u>, "when <u>I will make a new covenant</u> with the house of Israel and with the house of Judah, not like the covenant which I made with their fathers in the day I took them by the hand to bring them out of the land of Egypt, My covenant which they broke, although I was a husband to them," declares the Lord. "But this is the covenant which <u>I will make</u> with the house of Israel after those days," declares the Lord, "<u>I will</u> put My law within them, and on their heart <u>I will</u> write it; and <u>I will</u> be their God, and they shall be My people. And they shall not teach again, each man his neighbor and each man his brother, saying, 'Know the Lord,' for they shall all know Me, from the least of them to the greatest of them," declares the Lord, "for <u>I will</u> forgive their iniquity, and their sin <u>I will</u> remember no more."

First, I want you to notice that this is a *new* covenant. God said, *"Not like the covenant which I made with their fathers in the day I took them by the hand*

to bring them out of the land of Egypt." This covenant would be very different, and much better.

Next, we see that the Old Covenant had a problem.
*"My covenant <u>which they broke</u>, although I was a
husband to them," declares the Lord.* The problem
being that the children of Israel kept breaking the
covenant that they had made with God, (see Exodus
19-24). They kept turning their backs on God and
His commands. Every man did what was right in his
own eyes. So, do you think that the problem with the
Old Covenant would be the same problem with the
New Covenant? I do not think so, for how else could
God say it was better? Hebrews 8:6: *"But now He
[Christ] has obtained a more excellent ministry, by
as much as He is also the mediator of a <u>better cove-
nant</u>, which has been enacted on better promises."*

Take note of all the times God said, "I will," and
notice what He said He would do. Here is a list:

- I will put My law within them (v. 33).
- And on their heart, I will write it; My law (v.
  33; see also 2 Corinth. 3:2-3).
- I will be their God and they shall be My people
  (v. 33).
- They shall not teach again, each man his
  neighbor and each man his brother, saying,
  'Know the Lord,' for they shall all know Me,
  from the least of them to the greatest of them
  (v. 34; see also 1 Thess. 4:9; 1 John 2:27; John
  6:45).
- I will forgive their iniquity (v. 34).
- I will remember their sin no more (v. 34).

I hope you notice that some of these truths are also found in the New Testament. As you read the context surrounding these verses, it is plain to see that the letters were written to the Gentile believers too. Therefore, if some of the promises from the New Covenant are found in letters to Gentile believers, then we can safely assume that the rest of the promises in the New Covenant are theirs also. What do you think?

Now turn to Jeremiah 32:40: *"And I will make an everlasting covenant with them that I will not turn away from them, to do them good; and I will put the fear of Me in their hearts so that they will not turn away from Me."*

God said:

- I will make an everlasting covenant with them. This covenant will last forever. The Old Covenant was conditional. God said *if* you do these things *then* I will do such and such. But in the New Covenant God said, "I WILL." He does it, period!
- I will not turn away from them, to do them good.
- I will put the fear of Me in their hearts, so that *they will not turn away from Me.*

Do you remember what the problem was with the Old Covenant? Man kept breaking it; but here God said that He would put His fear *in* their hearts so that they *will not turn away from Him.* Keep in mind, it is God who puts His fear in man; this causes man *not* to walk away from God. Also in chapter four we saw in Romans 3:18: *"__There is no fear of God before their eyes__."* Please understand that unless God puts His fear *in* man, no man fears God.

Therefore, say to the house of Israel, "Thus says the Lord God, 'It is not for your sake, O house of Israel, that I am about to act, but for My holy name, which you have profaned among the nations where you went. And I will vindicate the holiness of My great name which has been profaned among the nations, which you have profaned in their midst. Then the nations will know that I am the Lord," declares the Lord God, "when I prove Myself holy among you in their sight. For I will take you from the nations, gather you from all the lands, and bring you into your own land. Then I will sprinkle clean water on you, and you will be clean; I will cleanse you from all your filthiness and from all your idols. Moreover, I will give you a new heart and put a new spirit within you; and I will remove the heart of stone from your flesh and give you a heart of flesh. And I will put My Spirit within you and cause you to walk in My statutes, and you will be careful to observe My ordinances" (Ezekiel 36:22-27).

Again, let us see what God said:

- I will vindicate the holiness of My great name, which you have profaned in their midst (verse 23).
- *I will* take you from the nations, and bring you into your own land (verse 24).
- *I will* sprinkle clean water on you, and you will be clean; *I will* cleanse you from all your filthiness and from all your idols (verse 25).
- *I will* give you a new heart (verse 26). When God saves our souls, we get a heart transplant. He gives us a brand new heart. This is a good thing, for in Jeremiah 17:9 God says this about the heart: ***"The heart is more deceitful than all else and is desperately sick; who can understand it?"*** God knew we needed a new heart.
- *I will* put a new spirit within you (verse 26). God puts a new spirit within all believers. This is different from His Holy Spirit. I believe this is a new nature. The word *new* here and in *new heart*, means, new as in fresh or better. Look at

2 Corinthians 5:17: ***"Therefore if any man is in Christ, he is a new creature; the old things passed away; behold, new things have come."*** The word *new* here has the same meaning as in Ezekiel; we become something *new* like being born again!

- *I will* remove the heart of stone from your flesh and give you a heart of flesh (verse 26).

- *I will put My Spirit within you and cause you to walk in My statutes,* and you will be careful to observe My ordinances (verse 2; see also John 7:38-39; 14:16-17).

In this last promise, God said He would put His Spirit within us. Let me ask a question: do you still think that the promises of the New Covenant are for another time, and only for the Jewish people? What do you believe about the Holy Spirit? When God saves a person, does His Spirit come into a man? God declared here that He would put His Spirit within you, He also said it in Joel 2:28-29: *"And it will come about after this that i will pour out My Spirit on all mankind; and your sons and daughters will prophesy, your old men will dream dreams, your young men will see visions. And even on the male and female servants I will pour out My Spirit in those days."* In Acts 2:16-18 Peter lets us know that this Scripture was being fulfilled the day of Pentecost.

Read with me in Galatians 3:13-14: *"Christ redeemed us from the curse of the Law, having become a curse for us—for it is written, 'Cursed is everyone who hangs on a tree' <u>in order that in Christ Jesus the blessing of Abraham might come to the Gentiles, so that we might receive the promise of the Spirit through faith</u>."* Do you see that? *In* Jesus Christ the blessing of Abraham, the promise of the Holy Spirit, came to the Gentile believers through faith. Again, if we find some of the promises mentioned in the New Covenant, like those in Jeremiah and Ezekiel, also made to the Gentile believers, then we have to agree that all the promises given in the New Covenant are for all believers! We cannot pick and choose; it is either all or nothing.

Look back to Ezekiel 36:27. God said He would put His Spirit *in man* and *this Holy Spirit causes man to walk (or live) in His statues.* It is only because of the Holy Spirit that man can keep God's statues and obey His words. Let's examine another Scripture that supports this, 2 Corinthians 3:4-9:

> *And such confidence we have through Christ toward God. Not that we are adequate in ourselves to consider anything as coming from ourselves, but our adequacy is from God, who also made us adequate as servants of a new covenant, not of the letter, but of the Spirit; for the letter kills, but the Spirit gives life. But if the ministry of death, in letters engraved on stones, came with glory, so that the sons of Israel could not look intently at the face of Moses because of the glory of his face, fading as it was, how shall the ministry of the Spirit fail to be even more with glory? For if the ministry of condemnation has glory, much more does the ministry of righteousness abound in glory.*

List:

- We are not adequate in ourselves.
- God makes believers adequate servants of the New Covenant by the Spirit.

- In this New Covenant we have the ministry of the Spirit and it is the ministry of righteousness.
- The law is referred to as ministry of death and the ministry of condemnation.

Here is a list of other things the Holy Spirit accomplishes for the believer:

1) The Holy Spirit gives life. John 6:63—*"It is the <u>Spirit who gives life</u>; the flesh profits nothing; the words that I have spoken to you are spirit and are life."*

2) We are born by the Spirit. John 3:6-8—*"That which is born of the flesh is flesh, and that which is <u>born of the Spirit</u> is spirit. Do not marvel that I said to you, 'You must be born again.' The wind blows where it wishes and you hear the sound of it, but do not know where it comes from and where it is going; so is everyone who is <u>born of the Spirit</u>."*

3) The Spirit teaches us all things. John 14:26—*"But <u>the Helper, the Holy Spirit</u>, whom <u>the Father will send in My name, He will teach you all things</u>, and bring to your remembrance all that I said to you."*

4) The Holy Spirit enables us to confess Jesus as Lord. First Corinthians 12:3— *"Therefore I make known to you, that no one speaking by the Spirit of God says, 'Jesus is accursed'; and no one can say, 'Jesus is Lord,' except by the Holy Spirit."*

5) The Holy Spirit bears witness to us, that we are children of God. Romans 8:16—*"The Spirit Himself bears witness with our spirit that we are children of God."*

6) The Holy Spirit also makes intercession for us. Romans 8:26—*"And in the same way the Spirit also helps our weakness; for we do not know how to pray as we should, but the Spirit Himself intercedes for us with groanings too deep for words."*

Of course, this is by no means a complete study of all that the Holy Spirit does for us but I hope it's enough to help you understand that the Spirit causes man to not only be born again, but to walk in such a way that pleases God. Man needed a helper and God sent us one. Now I hear some of you saying that we have a free will. We are not robots. Yes, this is true! But God sent us His helper, the Holy Spirit, to do just that, to help us, and His children welcome this.

Let's finish with the rest of the New Covenant. Hebrews 8:6-8—*"But now He has obtained a more excellent ministry, by as much as <u>He is also the mediator of a better covenant, which has been enacted on better promises. For if that first covenant had been faultless, there would have been no occasion sought for a second. For finding fault with them,</u> He says, 'Behold, days are coming, says the Lord, when I will effect a new covenant with the house of Israel and with the house of Judah.'"*

This Scripture tells us something more:

- Jesus has obtained a *more excellent* ministry.
- Jesus is the mediator of a *better covenant*. Hebrews 7:22 says, **"So _much the more_ also Jesus has become the guarantee of a better covenant."** In other words, Jesus is our mediator and He guarantees that the promises God made to believers in the New Covenant are carried out. He does this by the Holy Spirit. Praise God! He is the one who does the work in the believer's life. It is not up to us.
- The New Covenant has been enacted on *better promises*.
- *For if that first [covenant] had been aultless, there would have been no occasion sought for a second.*

Well, here you have it, the New Covenant. This is the reason, that when a person is truly saved, they will display evidence that proves they belong to God. God puts His laws in man's mind and writes them on his heart. Man begins to live a righteous life. Sin is dealt with by God right at the onset. Even before these people know what the Bible says is right or wrong, they begin to do the right things automatically. Why? Because God has written them on their hearts.

God also puts His fear in man, so that man will *not* turn away from Him. In the New Covenant, a true Christian will not forsake God or His Son Jesus. A true child of God will continue in the faith all the days of his life. Yes, we can become discouraged and want to quit on God like Jeremiah. Jeremiah 20:7-9— *"O Lord, Thou hast deceived me, and I was deceived; Thou hast overcome me and prevailed: I have become a laughing-stock all day long, everyone mocks me. For each time I speak, I cry aloud; I proclaim violence and destruction, because for me the word of the Lord has resulted in reproach and derision, all day long. But if I say, I will not remember Him, or speak anymore in His name, then in my heart it becomes like a burning fire shut up in my bones; and I am weary of holding it in, and I cannot endure it."* Even if we determine not to remember God any more, nor speak in His name again, our hearts become like a burning fire shut up in our bones and we cannot hold it in nor walk away from God.

God gives man a heart transplant. He gives us a new heart, and those who have entered into this covenant relationship with the one true God, receive also a new nature. We no longer have a sinful nature; *"And you were dead in your trespasses and sins, in which you formerly walked according to the course of this world, according to the prince of the power of the air, of the spirit that is now working in the sons of disobedience. Among them we too all formerly lived in the lusts of our flesh, indulging the desires of the flesh and of the mind, and were by nature children of wrath, even as the rest" (Ephesians 2:1-3).*

What we do have to contend with is the body of sin that Romans 6:5-6 speaks about. *"For if we have become united with Him in the likeness of His death, certainly we shall be also in the likeness of His resurrection. Knowing this, that our old self*

was crucified with Him, that <u>our body of sin</u> might be done away with, that we should no longer be slaves to <u>sin</u>." Please notice that in verse 6 we have three identities: 1) ***<u>our old self</u>*** 2) ***<u>our body of sin</u>*** 3) ***<u>sin</u>***, here personified as a master. Romans tell us that this old self was crucified with Christ. The word for, *crucified* means to be impale. Just like Christ, He was crucified and died, so too our old self, that old nature died, *never* to rise again. The problem we face is the body of sin. The Scriptures tell us that *the body of sin might be* done away *with*. The phrase *done away* (KJV uses the word *destroyed*) means to be useless. This body of sin, the flesh, no longer works the way it did before salvation. You could sort of say that it's broken now. Let me give you an illustration someone shared with me. Think of a puppet. Sin, as the master, controls the strings. The strings are the old self, our old nature, and the puppet is the body of sin. Before salvation, whatever the master (sin) wanted the puppet (body of sin) to do, he moved the strings (old self/old nature) and the puppet just followed along. But when a person truly becomes saved, the strings, the old self, are cut and destroyed. The puppet is still there but the control sin once had is gone. Yes, this body of sin is still very much alive and is hostile toward God. We will struggle, wrestle, and fight with our flesh till the day we die. That is why Romans 8:4b encourages us to, ***"walk not according to the flesh; but according to the Spirit."*** But because we are in the New Covenant, in place of the strings (the old self) we have a new nature, a new heart, instead of a heart of stone. We are possessed by the Spirit of the living God.

I know that there are many of you wondering about the fact that true believers do still commit sin, and how our spiritual growth plays into all this. Also, what about those that tragedy comes upon them or the people who experience such sorrow that their hearts never quite mend and they lose faith in God for a while? I will attempt to answer these questions.

First, let's talk about sin. When a person accepts Jesus Christ as Lord and Savior, they have a very large conscience that they did not have before God saved them. There is a *want* to please God and do right. As we begin our journey, God seems to deal with the big and obvious sins that have held us in slavery. He works more on the outside behavior. But as we continue, the focus moves to within us. God begins to address our motives, small white lies, sacrificing, watching what we say to others, and then kindness. He allows hard circumstances to test our faith and bring about godly character. Next, its love, unconditional love, the kind of love that makes us so vulnerable that it aches just to think about stepping out and forsaking self. He exposes root issues that cause our selfishness and He tears down all our defenses. This is a work of God. Yes, we can slow it down or speed it up as we wrestle with surrendering to the Holy Spirit, but I can't believe according to Scripture that one of God's true children can stop it, nor would they really want to.

Lastly, there are those who have experienced such sorrow and grief that they can't ever imagine trusting in a God who would allow such terrible things to happen. To this I can only share my story. I have walked with God for twenty-one years now, and as I'm writing this book I have just come out of my darkest days so far in my forty-nine years. I cannot share the details but I can say that the thing I had feared the most had come upon me. What had made the tragedy most painful was that I had prayed to God that He would not let it happen and yet He did.

I struggle more over the fact that God did not prevent the offence, than the offence itself, as horrible as it was. After serving God with all my heart; and yes, with all my shortcomings, weaknesses, and sins, I truly wanted to please God. Yet my heavenly Father did not intervene. I told God that I was done! I told Him I did not want to serve a God who would let this happen. I felt I no longer could trust Him. I know that for too many of you, this seems like blasphemy, but my Father let me pour out my heart, honestly and with no rebuke. The deepest and most heart-wrenching question I asked God was this, "You mean that You put this person on the altar to heal that person? What kind of God are You anyway?" I'll never forget His answer. He said, "The same God who put My Son on the altar for you!" This responds hit my heart hard, as I remembered God suffered over the injustice of His Child also.

I can't tell you that my pain or struggles went away; it's taken fourteen months now. I've struggled with depression and many times I just wanted to die. But not long after this all began, I believe I experienced what Abraham did in Genesis 15:12, "a terror and great darkness fell upon me." I saw my life without Jesus Christ and *that* pain swallowed up the other. I could not, I would not, live without my God. I realized that there is no pain too great, no broken heart too sorrowful, no disappointment so bad; no rejection so great that I would be willing to give up my God and Savior. So I ran back into His loving arms and cried like a baby. He took me up and rocked me for a long time.

Did I just tighten up my boots straps, suck it up, dust myself off, and get up? NO! I did not have the strength to get out of bed. But because my loving Father had entered into a covenant relationship me, He was determined to bring me through and carry me until I was able to walk again. It's interesting that I started this book almost four years ago and have struggled to finish it. I believe God has revealed these truths to me and through the Scriptures I feel I can defend them. But now, having gone through my greatest trial, I know them experientially. I wanted to walk away from God. I was done with Him. But because of His covenant, He had put His fear in me, I could not. Praise God! He wouldn't let me go.

John 6:39—*"And this is the will of Him [God] who sent Me [Jesus], that of ALL that He has given Me I lose NOTHING, but raise it up on the last day."*

John 10:27-29—*"My sheep hear My voice, and I know them, and they follow Me; and I give eternal life to them, and they shall never perish; and NO ONE shall snatch them out of My hand."*

For the love of Christ constrains us!

The New Covenant Promises

Jeremiah 31:31-34

    A) I will put My law within them (v. 33).

    B) And on their heart, I will write it [My law] (v. 33; see also 2 Corth. 3:2-3).

    C) I will be their God (v. 33).

    D) And they shall be My people (v. 33).

    E) They shall not teach again, each man his neighbor and each man his brother, saying, 'Know the Lord,' for they shall all know Me, from the least of them to the greatest of them (v. 34; see also, 1 Thess. 4:9; 1 John 2:27; John 6:45).

    F) I will forgive their iniquity (v. 34).

    G) I will remember their sin no more (v. 34).

Jeremiah 32:40

    H) I will make an everlasting covenant with them.

    I) I will not turn away from them, to do them good.

    J) I will put the fear of Me in their hearts, so that *they will not turn away from Me.*

Ezekiel 36:22-27

    K) I will vindicate the holiness of My great name, which you have profaned in their midst.

    L) *I will* take you from the nations, and bring you into your own land.

M) *I will* sprinkle clean water on you, and you will be clean; *I will* cleanse you from all your filthiness and from all your idols.

N) *I will* give you a new heart.

O) *I will* put a new spirit within you.

P) *I will* remove the heart of stone from your flesh and give you a heart of flesh.

Q) *I will put My Spirit within you and cause you to walk in My statutes*, and you will be careful to observe My ordinances.

Luke 22:17-20

R) Jesus is telling us here, ***"This cup which is poured out for you is the new* covenant in My blood."**

2 Corinthians 3:4-9

S) God makes believers adequate servants of the New Covenant by the Spirit.

T) The New Covenant is also called the ministry of the Spirit and the ministry of righteousness.

U) The law is referred to as the ministry of death and the ministry of condemnation.

Hebrews 8:6-13

V) Jesus has obtained a *more excellent ministry*.

W) Jesus is the mediator of a *better covenant*.

X) The New Covenant has been enacted on *better promises*.

Y) The New Covenant is faultless.

You search the Scriptures,
because you think that in
them you have
eternal life;
and it is these that bear
witness of Me.
                              John 5:39

What Do You Believe?
Part Seven

So what do *you* believe? The word, *believe* means *to place your trust in something or someone.* Most people believe what they've been taught. If you attend a certain church for any length of time you begin to take on their doctrines. Some churches believe in eternal salvation. Others do not. One of these is wrong and that's just one subject. There are hundreds of promises in the Bible. How can you claim them if your truth comes from others?

Have you taken the time to search the Scriptures for yourself? 2 Timothy 2:15 encourages us to, ***"Be diligent to present yourselves approved to God as a workman who does not need to be ashamed, handling accurately the word of truth."*** Are you rightly handling God's Word? Do not trust another person's opinion on critical matters. What if they are wrong? Remember, heaven and hell, hang in the balance!

On the other hand, let's say what you do believe is true. Can you prove it to someone? I don't mean to take a Scripture here and there, but to flow through the Word of God and prove a truth. 2 Timothy 1:12 says, ***"For this reason I also suffer these things, but I am not ashamed; <u>for I know whom I have believed and I am convinced that He is able to guard what I have entrusted to Him</u> until that day."*** Paul knew whom he believed in—Jesus, and he was *convinced* that He was able to keep all he entrusted to Him. What about you? Can you say that? Do you want to be able to?

I would like to turn to a familiar Scripture, Luke 15:11-32, the story of the prodigal son. Most of us have heard many sermons on this parable. In fact, there are at least two different beliefs concerning this passage. 1) Some believe that the prodigal son is a true child of God and that sometime after salvation, he walks away from God, goes out into the world, and squanders his money on loose living. In another words, he is backslidden. 2) Others believe that this young man was never saved to start with. Which doctrine have you heard? What do you believe about him and this Scripture?

The first rule we must remember when studying the Bible, after praying, is to *always* leave the Scripture in its *context*. Most people will go straight to the verses that they want to study and bypass the verses that surround it. We must look for some starting point and begin our study there. In the case of the prodigal son we must start at verse one of Luke 15. The reason for this is that Jesus did not just tell one parable but three. We find Him talking to a group of people, and He is trying to teach them a truth. So He goes from one parable to another. We can be certain that the truth He is trying to teach is the same in all three parables, because there is no break in His story. Also, all three of the parables have the same repeated words.

Come and see.

Read Luke 15:1-3—*"Now all the tax-gatherers and the sinners were coming near Him to listen to Him. And both the Pharisees and the scribes began to grumble, saying, 'This man receives sinners and eats with them.' And He told them this parable, saying…"*

When we begin we must look for the obvious, clear repeated truth. Then ask questions, and of course, make lists.

Who was present when Jesus was talking? *Tax-gathers, sinners, Pharisees, and scribes.* This can be broken into two categories: sinners and the religious.

Jesus told them a parable. A parable means to place one thing beside another, to compare them.

In verses 1-2, who was coming close to Jesus to hear Him? *Tax-gatherers and sinners.*

What was the Pharisees' and scribes' response? *They grumbled saying, "This man receives sinners and eats with them."* Remember this. We will come back to this at the end of the story.

Now read Luke 15:4-7:

What man among you, if he has a hundred sheep and has lost one of them, does not leave the ninety-nine in the open pasture, and go after the one which is lost, until he finds it? And when he has found it, he lays it on his shoulders, rejoicing. And when he comes home, he calls together his friends and his neighbors, saying to them, "Rejoice with me, for I have found my sheep which was lost!" I tell you that in the same way, there will be more joy in heaven over one sinner who repents, than over ninety-nine righteous persons who need no repentance.

What is the problem? *There's a lost sheep.*

What does the man do? *He goes after the one which is lost until He finds it.*

Then when he finds it, what does he do? *He calls together his friends and his neighbors, saying, "Rejoice with me, for I have found my sheep which was lost."*

Is this man just a little excited or is he throwing a party? It sounds like he is having a major party to me.

In verse 7, let's look at what Jesus compares this to. *"I tell you that in the same way, there will be more joy in heaven over one sinner who repents, than over ninety-nine righteous persons who need no repentance."*

The word *sinner* in verses 7 and 10 means an unregenerate man. He is spiritually dead. The word *repents* in verses 7 and 10 means to change one's mind and direction, always for the better. This is the same word both Jesus (Matthew 4:17) and John the Baptist (Matthew 3:2) used in preaching to the lost that the kingdom of heaven was at hand.

What are some *key words*? *Sinner, lost, found, rejoice, and repent.*

Now read Luke 15:8-10—*"Or what woman, if she has ten silver coins and loses one coin, does not light a lamp and sweep the house and search care-fully until she finds it? And when she has found it, she calls together her friends and neighbors, saying, "Rejoice with me, for I have found the coin which I had lost!" In the same way, I tell you, there is joy in the presence of the angels of God over one sinner who repents."*

What was the problem? There is a *lost coin.*

What does the woman do*? She lights a lamp and sweeps the house and searches carefully until she finds it.*

What happens when she finds it? *She calls together her friends and neighbors, saying, "Rejoice with me, for I have found the coin which I had lost."*

How is this lady celebrating the coin she found? She also throws a big party.

What does Jesus compare this to? *"In the same way, I tell you, there is joy in the presence of the angels of God over one sinner who repents."* This verse, as well as verse 7, is very similar. When Jesus repeats Himself, He really wants us to *hear!* Sandwiched between these three parables we find two power statements. Heaven rejoices over one **sinner**, over a godless man becoming saved.

What are the key words for this parable? *Sinner, lost, found, rejoice, and repent.*

Do you think that parable one and two sound alike? Absolutely! Not only do they have the same repeated words, the themes in both are alike. The most interesting item they have in common is Jesus' statements at the end of both.

Now read Luke 15:11-17:

And He said, "A certain man had two sons; and the younger of them said to his father, 'Father, give me the share of the estate that falls to me.' And he divided his wealth between them. And not many days later, the younger son gathered everything together and went on a journey into a distant country, and there he squandered his estate with loose living. Now when he had spent everything, a severe famine occurred in that

*country, and he began to be in need. And
he went and attached himself to one of the
citizens of that country, and he sent him into
his fields to feed swine. And he was longing
to fill his stomach with the pods that the
swine were eating, and no one was giving
anything to him. But when he came to his
senses, he said, 'How many of my father's
hired men have more than enough bread,
but I am dying here with hunger!'"*

Between Luke 15:10-11, has Jesus changed His
location, or is He talking to a different group of
people? No, Jesus is at the same place and His hearers
have not changed. His conversation is continuing.

In verses 11-17, how does this story unfold? A
father had two sons. The younger asked for his part
of the inheritance and left town. What happened to
him? He spent everything on loose living, and found
himself broke, and hungry.

What happened in verse 17? *He came to his
senses.* This is a very good thing!

Read Luke 15:18-24:

*I will get up and go to my father, and will
say to him, "Father, I have sinned against
heaven, and in your sight; I am no longer
worthy to be called your son; make me as
one of your hired men." And he got up and
came to his father. But while he was still a
long way off, his father saw him, and felt
compassion for him, and ran and embraced*

him, and kissed him. And the son said to him, "Father, I have sinned against heaven and in your sight; I am no longer worthy to be called your son." But the father said to his slaves, "Quickly bring out the best robe and put it on him, and put a ring on his hand and sandals on his feet; and bring the fattened calf, kill it, and let us eat and be merry; for this son of mine was dead, and has come to life again; he was lost, and has been found." And they began to be merry.

What does he declare that he will say when he sees his father? **"Father I have sinned against heaven and in your sight, I am no longer worthy to be called your son."**

What does that sound like to you? I think the young man is considering repentance.

What does he say when he gets home? *"Father I have sinned against heaven and in your sight, I am no longer worthy to be called your son."*

Would you call this *repentance*? *Yes!*

What happens next? The father clothes his son and makes a feast for him.

Would you say he was rejoicing? YES! He is throwing a great big party! He killed the fatted calf and all. Is some of this sounding familiar to you?

Our *key words* so far in this parable have been *sinned, lost, and found.* Although the words *repent* and *rejoice* are not found here, it is clear that those actions are. Remember, these are the same key words found in the other two parables. Interesting isn't it!

Verse 24 tells us something more about this young man. What is it? ***"For this son of mine was <u>dead and has come to life again</u>."*** Now wait a minute. Was there an accident? Did I miss something? When did this man die? Let's look at these two words.

This word *dead*, means spiritually dead, lost, and without God.

The phrase *has come to life again* means *to revive* or *to live again.* Remember what happened to Adam? At the beginning Adam was alive both physically and spiritually. Since all men were *in* Adam, that was everyone's condition too. Then Adam died spiritually because of his failure to trust and obey God. On that day all men died too.

This son was spiritually dead, he then came to his senses, repented, and became born again. He was *not* a believer who had backslidden and had come back to God. This son was *never* born again to start with, as with the other parables in this Scripture—lost sheep, lost coin, and lost son. If we leave this Scripture in its context we can have only one interpretation. The son in this parable was lost but he did repent and became born again, a true child of God.

Let's finish, Luke 15:25-32:

Now his older son was in the field, and when he came and approached the house, he heard music and dancing. And he summoned one of the servants and began inquiring what these things might be. And he said to him, "Your brother has come, and your father has killed the fattened calf, because he has received him back safe and sound." But he became angry, and was not willing to go in; and his father came out and began entreating him. But he answered and said to his father, "Look! For so many years I have been serving you, and I have never neglected a command of yours; and yet you have never given me a kid, that I might be merry with my friends; but when this son of yours came, who has devoured your wealth with harlots, you killed the fattened calf for him." And he said to him, "My child, you have always been with me, and all that is mine is yours. But we had to be merry and rejoice, for this brother of yours was dead and has begun to live, and was lost and has been found."

Here we have a son mad and complaining over a party his father has thrown for a lost son who has come home. Remember at the beginning of the chapter what was happening?

Luke 15:1-2: **"Now all the tax-gatherers and the sinners were coming near Him to listen to Him. And both the Pharisees and the scribes began to <u>grumble</u>, saying, "This man receives sinners and eats with them."** I believe that Jesus is comparing this bitter son to the Pharisees and scribes. They also had a problem with Jesus who received and ate with sinners. I'm sure they realized what Jesus meant.

The Scripture mentioning "a father having two sons" throws some people. They reason that if he was the father of both sons, they both must be saved. Some passages, such as Ephesians 4:6 and 1 Corinthians 8:6 refer to God as the Father of all mankind, lost and saved.

The word *prodigal* is not found anywhere in the inspired Word of God. We do have it as a heading, but not in the actual Scriptures. The word *prodigal* means reckless and out of control. So how did this parable come to be known as that of the prodigal son instead of the parable of the lost son? I don't know!

Did you see anything new from our study? Do you now see clearly what this parable is about? All we did was keep it in context and let the Scriptures interpret themselves.

We're not finished here yet. Let's look at another angle of believing. We were just talking about Adam and the fall. Remember that Adam had failed to trust (believe) in God and in turn did not obey Him. Keep in mind Adam walked and talked to God, so it wasn't like he needed to believe if God existed or not, but would he trust His word and the things He said. Until a person can trust God and take Him at His word, he will never obey Him. Obedience reveals that we trust God.

The Scripture says in Hebrews 11:6, *"And without faith it is impossible to please Him, for he who comes to God must believe that He is, and that He is a rewarder of those who seek Him."* Do you believe His Word? If so, have you submitted to His authority? Have you bowed the knee to the One who so graciously paid the price for your sins? These are questions that need to be answered.

Concerning this issue of lordship, there are some who teach that we can pray a prayer and make Jesus our Savior and not obey His words. You know, have a one-way ticket to heaven, and yet not tied to a bunch of rules. This teaching also states that a person can even walk away from God for some extended periods and then years later, come to the realization that Jesus truly deserves to be Lord of our lives. At this point, we begin serving Him, becoming free from sin, and able to love Him and others. In short, this teaching says that we can be saved, but not make Jesus our Lord, yet we keep full control of our lives and all along, are sure that we are saved.

We will look at some passages and decide for ourselves. Turn to Romans 10:9-10—*"That if you <u>confess</u> with your mouth <u>Jesus as Lord</u>, and <u>believe in your heart</u> that God raised Him from the dead, <u>you shall be saved</u>; for <u>with the heart man believes, resulting in righteousness, and with the mouth he confesses, resulting in salvation</u>."*

The first thing we notice is the confession. Jesus is Lord! Throughout the Bible, God has revealed His names to man at different times to show His attributes. When Abraham needed a sacrifice in Genesis 22, God made Himself known as Jehovah-jireh, my provider. We know that God does not haphazardly put words together. So we must conclude that there is a specific reason the Holy Spirit had these two words back to back.

Let's do a word search on them. First, Jesus. Turn to Matthew 1:21—*"And she will bear a Son; and <u>you shall call His name Jesus, for it is He who will</u>*

_**save His people from their sins**_*."* We see the name of Jesus is connected to Savior, He who will save His people from their sins. When we say Jesus, it is not just His name, it means Savior of the world.

Now for the name *Lord*, it means having power or authority over someone. It means a master or owner of someone. Someone you *willingly* entrust yourself to.

These two words are inseparable. The Word says, *"If you _**confess**_ with your mouth _**Jesus as Lord**_."* The word, *confess* means that *you agree with God* about who He says His Son is. He is both Savior of the world and has all power and authority.

Ephesians 1:20-22—*"**Which He [God] brought about in Christ, when He raised Him from the dead, and seated Him at His right hand in the heavenly places, far above all rule and authority and power and dominion, and every name that is named, not only in this age, but also in the one to come. And He put all things in subjection under His feet, and gave Him as head over all things to the church.**"*

So the biggest question you will ever answer is this: have you accepted Jesus as your personal Savior, the one who will save you from your sins, **AND** as your Master, the one who is in control over your life? Have you bowed the knee to Him? Read with me, Philippians 2:9-11—*"**Therefore also God highly exalted Him, and bestowed on Him the name which is above every name, that _at the name of Jesus every knee should bow_, of those who are _in heaven_, and _on earth_, and _under the earth_, and that**"*

every tongue should confess that JESUS CHRIST IS LORD, to the glory of God the Father."
Understand this: you can either bow the knee now or later but do not be mistaken. Every knee *will bow* to Jesus some day and confess Him as Lord. This is who He is, and it makes no difference if people believe it, acknowledge it, or accept it, **Jesus is Lord**. The question is, is He yours?

Let's get back to Romans 10:9: ***"If you confess with your mouth Jesus as Lord, and believe in your heart that God raised Him from the dead, you shall be saved."*** Notice it says, "*believe in your heart*." It does not say, "If you confess with your mouth Jesus as Lord and *believe in your head* that God raised Him from the dead you shall be saved." There is a *big* difference between your head and your heart. Your heart is all of your being, your will, mind, emotions, and personality. Therefore, when you believe these truths with your heart, you will be saved. God is searching for more depth than what occurs in the intellect. He wants us to believe with our hearts.

I struggled trying to understand the difference between believing with the head or the heart. The two appear to be so interrelated. I wanted to know the difference, because although there is about twelve inches between the two, only one will take you to heaven! So I prayed and asked God to help me understand this truth. He had someone share a word picture, a story, with me. I would like to share it with you. Maybe it will help you understand too.

There once was a man that used to tightrope across many high places. One time he strung his cable across the Grand Canyon. He had a large crowd of spectators on both sides. Before he began his first attempt he turned to the people behind him and asked, "Do you believe that I can walk on this wire to the other side?" The crowd responded with loud cheers and said, "Of course we believe! We've seen you in action."

So with his balance stick in hand, he headed across the wire, ever so cautiously. When he reached the other side, the crowd went nuts. They were shouting and cheering! He then turned to the crowd on that side, and once they were calm enough to hear him, he asked the same question, "Do you believe I can walk the tightrope back?" The crowd seemed a little puzzled but then people started shouting, "Yes! Yes we believe you can!" For the crowd it almost seemed like a no-brainer. They had already watched him perform the act. He went back to the other side. Again, he arrived safely and the crowd roared and applauded.

At this point, the man had someone hand him a wheelbarrow. It was a special one, made for his cable. He turned to the onlookers and asked, "What about now? Do you believe I can do this while pushing a wheelbarrow?" For just a few seconds the crowd was silent, as they thought about it, then they broke out with shouts, "Yes, we believe you can!" That's what he was waiting for, so he went across the Grand Canyon with his wheelbarrow. When he reached the other side, people were beside themselves. They laughed and cheered for quite some time.

Finally, when everything calmed down the man looked at the crowd and asked, "Do you believe I can do that again?" The people shouted their loudest, "Yes, of course we believe!" The man waited for the crowd to calm down and the next moment he asked, "OK, who wants to get into the wheelbarrow?" What, silence. There was total silence. No one moved; everyone was shocked by the question. In fact, after a few moments people began to leave quietly. No one volunteered for this adventure.

What happened to these people? They seemed convinced that he could do what he had said. The problem was they believed with their heads, not their hearts. No one *really* trusted him. When they were put to the test, the results proved they did not believe in him at all. It was easy to be on the sidelines and shout, "We believe" *when it did not cost them anything*.

I am convinced it's always been this same way with people. It is easy for us to say, "Yes, we believe in Jesus." However, when it comes down to truly trusting Him, when there is a cost involved, we do not move. We are frozen with fear. The Bible says in Romans 10:9 that, ***"If you <u>confess</u> with your mouth <u>Jesus as Lord</u>, and <u>believe in your heart</u> that God raised Him from the dead, <u>you shall be saved</u>."*** When you confess Jesus as Lord *and* believe in your *heart* that God raised Him from the dead, *then you shall be saved*. If you ignore one thing in this Scripture, you shall *not* be saved.

Now let's look at the rest of that Scripture. Romans 10:10, states, ***"For with <u>the heart man</u>***

believes, resulting in righteousness, and with the mouth he confesses, resulting in salvation." When we truly believe these facts with our heart, and we climb into the wheelbarrow, it produces righteousness within us. Know this for sure, that this righteousness is not ours but Christ's. Nevertheless, we will begin to live a righteous life. How does this happen? Remember the New Covenant? When a person enters into a covenant relationship with the living God, God writes His laws in their hearts. He also puts the Holy Spirit in them and causes them to walk according to His ways.

In conclusion remember these facts:

- We must confess and make Jesus our Lord and Savior.
- We must believe God raised Him from the dead.
- This belief occurs in the heart, not the head.
- Then we are saved.
- We begin to live right as a result.

When we come to the end of ourselves and realize our need for someone greater than ourselves, the heart is ripe and ready for a redeemer. If we trust in God and believe what He says, we will *obey* Him. John 3:36 expresses the same thought: ***"He who believes in the Son has eternal life; but he who does not obey the Son shall not see life, but the wrath of God abides on him."***

133

Acts 4:12— *"And there is salvation in no one else; for there is no other name under heaven that has been given among men, by which we must be saved." JESUS the CHRIST!*

*Jesus answered and
said to him,
"Truly, truly, I say
to you unless one
is born again
he cannot see the
kingdom of God."*
John 3:3

Born Again
Part Eight

B orn again, what exactly does that mean? Jesus
tells us in John 3 that *"unless a person is born
again he cannot see the kingdom of God."* Since
a person must be born again in order to make it to
heaven, we need to know what this means, how it
happens, and most importantly, how a person can
know they are born again! Being assured of your
salvation is too important to take lightly. Please do

not take anybody else's word and hope that they are right, not your parents, your Sunday school teacher, your pastor, your spouse, or your best friend. This issue is really just between you and God. You can settle it here in this life or you can wait and find out what is true when you die. That would be an eternal mistake if you are wrong.

You might know the truth and know that you possess eternal life. Nevertheless, you and other truly born-again Christians still need to know these truths. Why? Because I want to challenge you in what you have been taught versus what the Bible really says about salvation.

I believe that this generation of evangelicals has committed a gross atrocity, in that we have preached a cheap salvation. A salvation, that has taken grace, and as Jude 4 states, "has turned the grace of God into licentiousness." Ask yourself if that is what you think when you are singing that precious song *Amazing Grace*. I do not think so, nor was it the author's intention. Grace is the God-given ability to run our race and finish it.

Quoting Ephesians 1:3—*"Blessed be the God and Father of our Lord Jesus Christ, who has blessed us with EVERY spiritual blessings in the heavenly places IN Christ."* And 2 Peter 1:2-3—*"Grace and peace be multiplied to you in the knowledge of God and of Jesus our Lord, seeing that His divine power has granted to us EVERYTHING pertaining to life and godliness, through the <u>true knowledge of Him</u> who called us by His own glory and excellence."*

I have heard many people say, "We are no longer under the law. We are now under grace." Ask the next person who says that, "What do you mean"? Are they saying that the God of all creation, who hates sin so much, that He sent His Son to suffer a terrible death to satisfy the penalty of sin, and now, once a person is saved, that He somehow overlooks it and turns His head? NEVER! That mindset is a direct contradiction to the very nature of God. We have already seen much Scripture which confirms that Christ's work on the cross was to deal with sin and free man from bondage. *"If the Son shall make you free, you shall be free indeed" (John 8:36).*

I'll get off my soapbox for now and get back to subject at hand—being born again. Let us look in John 3:3. *"Jesus answered and said to him, "Truly, truly, I say to you, unless one is born again, he cannot see the kingdom of God.'"* If man is to see God and His kingdom, we must be born again. The word *again* means *from above*, meaning you must be born from heaven. Jesus helps us understand this term in verses 1-8 where Jesus is having a conversation with a man named Nicodemus.

Now there was a man of the Pharisees, named Nicodemus, a ruler of the Jews; this man came to Him by night, and said to Him, "Rabbi, we know that You have come from God as a teacher; for no one can do these signs that You do unless God is with him." Jesus answered and said to him, "Truly, truly, I say to you, unless one is born *again, he cannot see the kingdom of God." Nicodemus said to Him, "How can a man be born when he is old? He cannot enter a second time into his mother's womb and be born, can he?" Jesus answered, "Truly, truly, I say to you, <u>unless one is born of water and the Spirit, he cannot enter into the kingdom of God</u>. That which is born of the flesh is flesh, and <u>that which is born of the Spirit is spirit</u>. Do not marvel that I said to you, '<u>You must be born again</u>.' The wind blows where it wishes and you hear the sound of it, but do not know where it comes from and where it is going; so is everyone who is born of the Spirit."*

During the course of this discussion, we find that Jesus and Nicodemus are actually talking about two very different kinds of births; the natural birth and the spiritual birth:

Natural Birth	**Spiritual Birth**
• Can a man be born when he is old	• You must be born again
• Unless born of water (natural)	• Born of water (natural) and of the Spirit (spiritual).
• that which is born of flesh is flesh	• That which is born of Spirit is spirit.

Jesus is talking about a spiritual birth. No one knows exactly how this happens but Jesus compares it to the wind. *"The wind blows where it wishes and you hear the sound of it, but do not know where it comes from and where it is going; so is everyone who is born of the Spirit" (3:8).* I do not know how or when the tumblers of a soul all click in place and this birth occur, but the effects afterward will be clearly seen!

Read what the Scriptures say about a person born of God:

1) John 1:12-13—*"But as many as received Him, to them He gave the right to become <u>children of God</u>, even to those who believe in His name, who were born not of blood, nor of the will of the flesh, nor of the will of man, but of God."* Man is born of God, not of his own will! The work is God's, not ours! Is this not the same as with our children? They did *nothing* to help the process of birth to take place.

2) 1 John 2:29—*"If you know that He is righteous, you know that everyone also who <u>practices righteousness is born of Him</u>."* This verse states that when one is truly born of God, they will practice righteousness.

3) 1 John 3:1-11— *See how great a love the Father has bestowed upon us, that we should be called <u>children of God</u>; and such we are. For this reason the world does not know us, because it did not know Him. Beloved, <u>now we are children of God</u>, and it has not appeared as yet what we shall be. We know*

that, when He appears, we shall be like Him, because we shall see Him just as He is. And <u>everyone who has this hope fixed on Him purifies himself</u>, just as He is pure. Everyone <u>who practices sin also practices lawlessness</u>; and sin is lawlessness. And YOU KNOW THAT HE APPEARED IN ORDER TO TAKE AWAY SINS; and in Him there is no sin. No one who abides in Him sins; no one who sins has seen Him or knows Him. Little children, LET NO ONE DECEIVE YOU; the one who practices righteousness is righteous, just as He is righteous; the one who practices sin is of the devil; for the devil has sinned from the beginning. The Son of God appeared for this purpose, that He might destroy the works of the devil. <u>No one who is born of God practices sin</u>, because His seed abides in him; and he cannot sin, because he is born of God. No one who abides in Him sins; <u>By this the children of God and the children of the devil are obvious:</u> anyone who does not practice righteousness is not of God, nor the one who does not love his brother.

This Scripture is exposing a major contrast between the children of God and the children of the devil. Let's make a chart and see what it reveals to us.

The Children of God	Children of the devil
• Can a man be born when he is old	• the one who *practices* sin also *practices* lawlessness (v. 4)
• when He appears, we shall be like Him (v. 2)	• no one who sins has seen Him or knows Him (v. 6)
• everyone who has this hope [fixed] on Him one who sins has seen purifies himself (v. 3)	• the one who *practices* sin is of devil (v. 8)
• he who *practices* righteousness is righteous (v. 7)	• anyone who does NOT practice righteousness is not of God, nor the one who does *not* love (v. 10)
• *no one* "born of God" *practices sin,* because God's SEED abides *in* him and he cannot sin because he is born of God (v. 9)	

By this the children of God and the children of the devil are obvious (v. 10).

Some Scripture has so much clearly repeated truth that you can't explain it away; 1 John is one of them. A child born of God will *practice* righteousness not unrighteousness. If a person *does not* practice righteousness he is *not* a child of God.

Now because some of the verses found in 1 John 3 are difficult to understand, many have come to their own conclusions that do not follow the context. Let's look and see what I am talking about: 3:6— *No one who abides in Him sins; no one who sins has seen Him or knows Him.* And 3:9—*No one who is born of God practices sin, because His seed abides in him; and he cannot sin, because he is born of God.* Please notice these two underlined phrases. Many people say that this Scripture must *not* be really talking about *sin* because true believers in Jesus Christ do sin. I do agree that true believers sin, in fact, 1 John 2:1-2 agrees with that statement: *"My little children, I am writing these things to you that you may not sin. And if anyone sins, we have an Advocate with the Father, Jesus Christ the righteous; and He Himself is the propitiation for our sins; and not for ours only, but also for those of the whole world."*

Nevertheless, sandwiched in these verses, is the word *practice.* Here, it is used five times. The word *practice* is something you do over and over. The Scripture is giving us clearly repeated truth; no one born of God has a lifestyle of sin. It *does not mean* that children of God cannot sin; *we can and do commit acts of sin* as 1 John 2:1-2 just told us.

According to the context we will *not* practice sin, meaning that our lifestyle will not reflect a constant sinning. We might lie but we won't be known as liars. Or we might have an affair but immorality will not be the standard throughout our days. Consider King David; he had an affair with another man's wife. Yet we can look over his life and although it was not perfect we do not see him ever committing that sin again, and again.

If your life is sprinkled with the same constant sin, then follow Paul's advice *"Test yourselves to see if you are in the faith; examine yourselves! Or do you not recognize this about yourselves, that Jesus Christ is in you—unless indeed you fail the test? But I trust that you will realize that we ourselves do not fail the test."* 2 Corinth. 13:5-6

Why can't a true child of God continue a life of sin? Because *His seed abides in him; and he cannot sin, because he is born of God (1 John 3:9).* 2 Corinthians 5:17 tells us, *"Therefore if any man is in Christ, he is a new creature; the old things passed away; behold, new things have come."* When we are truly born again we really do become a new creation in Christ. I have an awesome picture in my house of a beautiful butterfly that has just emerged from its cocoon. It does not have any resemblance to the caterpillar it once was. Such is the new birth.

I believe that since our modern western religious culture has failed to realize the need to search the Scriptures for ourselves, and most who stand behind the pulpits in this country just tickle the ears of their hearers, we've not been challenged to make sure we are saved. Unfortunately, this has left many to rest on a false hope, distributed by a watered down, counterfeit gospel. It will never be a simple process, this wrestling with our souls, but one that each of us must undertake for our assurance. The first step is to measure our lives by the Word of God

Let me share what I think takes place in many of our churches. The message is preached and people are invited to come forward and pray the sinner's prayer. They are told that they are now saved. I believe that a large majority of these people never got it. Let me ask you a question. Whenever a man and woman come together and have intercourse, and a conception occurs, does a birth always take place? No! Many times a birth does not take place: the mother can miscarry, have an abortion, or even have a stillbirth. So just because a conception has taken place, it *does not* mean that a birth will! I think this same principle holds true with spirituality. Jesus tells us that we must be born again, so before a birth can take place, there must first be a conception. I am convinced that many people mistake this spiritual conception for the new birth. They then cling to their experience.

John 6:44 says, ***"No one can come to Me, unless the Father who sent Me draws him; and I will raise him up on the last day."*** We do not get saved when we are ready. Salvation can only happen when God the Father draws us. Like we saw in the Sower and the Seed, men can hear the gospel and even respond to it and still salvation not take place.

Can a person become born again the first time they hear the gospel? Yes, I believe so, but I am convinced that many times a spiritual conception, not the new birth, is what happens. When a true birth does occur, you and all those around you will be able to tell it.

Let me pause here. I do not want anyone to misunderstand this analogy and compare it to the sanctity of life and the fight for the unborn children. I, like all Christians, believe that life begins at the moment of conception! So please do not get the wrong impression here and let me lose you with this word picture.

Have you ever been around a young couple that has no children? Their lifestyle is set, they have a routine, even the house is arranged in a particular order. Then one day they bring a baby home. Everything from that day forward will be different. All their friends, family, and neighbors will know that a baby has been born and has invaded this young couple's life. The same is true with a spiritual birth; when it is *real*, all those around you will notice the drastic change that has taken place. There is a baby in the house.

How long can it be between a spiritual conception and a spiritual birth? I don't know. It could be years. Sadly, many have a spiritual miscarriage before a true birth takes place. They have walked an aisle, prayed a prayer, and believed the facts about Jesus, but nothing has changed.

I've even heard pastors tell people who have come forward and prayed the sinner's prayer that, "Now you are saved, and in a year or two *if the devil comes and tells you* that you are not saved, you go back to *this day*." To me, that is so wrong. First, how can anyone know that a person got saved? Remember it's a heart issue and you and I are not capable of reading a man's heart. That's God's job. But what if it's not the devil talking? What if it's the Holy Spirit trying to bring a person to a true saving knowledge of Jesus? And secondly, there is no place in the Bible that tells us that our assurance is in the *day* that you walked an aisle and made a profession. What the Bible does tell us over and over is to examine our lives and see what kind of fruit is there.

God has blessed me with five beautiful children: Jay, Brandy, Joe, Kerri, and Natalie. Since Natalie was the baby, I was feeling the empty nest syndrome early on, so when she was old enough to talk with me, I would ask her not to grow up. She, of course, promised me that she wouldn't. However, as the years went by she broke her promise and I would often say, "Nat, you lied to me, you're growing up." With the most sincere look she would say, "I'm sorry Mom, I'm trying not to, but I just can't help it."

The same is true of those born of God. They will grow and have fruit. Yes, some more than others but there will be fruit/proof in the life of every believer.

Let's look at some more passages on those born of God:

1) 1 John 4:7—*"Beloved, let us love one another, for love is from God; and everyone who loves is born of God and knows God."* If we are born of God, we *will* love one another and *know* Him, meaning we will truly be saved.

2) 1 John 5:1-5, 18— *Whoever believes that Jesus is the Christ is <u>born of God</u>; and whoever loves the Father loves the child born of Him. By this we know that we love the <u>chil-</u>*

> **dren of God, when we love God and observe
> His commandments. For this is the love of
> God, that we keep His commandments; and
> His commandments are not burdensome.
> For whatever is born of God overcomes the
> world; and this is the victory that has over-
> come the world—our faith. And who is the
> one who overcomes the world, but he who
> believes that Jesus is the Son of God? We
> know that no one who is born of God sins;
> but He who was born of God keeps him and
> the evil one does not touch him.**

Once again, we have clearly repeated truth about
those who are born of God:

- Whoever believes that Jesus is the Christ is
  born of God.
- Whoever loves the Father loves the [child]
  born of Him.
- By this, we know that we love the children
  of God; when we love God and observe His
  commandments.
- This is the love of God, that we keep His
  commandments.
- Whatever is *born of God* overcomes the world;
  and this is the victory that has overcome the
  world—our faith.
- Who overcomes the world; but he who believes
  that Jesus is the Son of God?
- We know that no one who is *born of God* sins
  (a lifestyle of sinning).

- He who was *born of God* keeps him and the evil one does not touch him.

I do not know how much Scripture people need to be convinced how those born of God will behave, but these are clear. Those who are truly God's children *will* love God, Jesus, and His children. They *will* observe and keep God's commands. They *will* overcome the world by their faith. They *will not* have a lifestyle of sin, nor will they hate their brothers and sisters in Christ.

Look at these Scriptures:

3) John 3:21—*"But he who practices the truth comes to the light, that his deeds may be manifested as having been wrought in God."*
4) Hebrews 7:22—*"So much the more also Jesus has become the guarantee of a better covenant."*
5) Phil. 1:6—*"For I am confident of this very thing, that He who began a good work in you will perfect it until the day of Christ Jesus."*
6) Hebrews 12:2—*"Fixing our eyes on Jesus, the author and perfecter of faith, who for the joy set before Him endured the cross, despising the shame, and has sat down at the right hand of the throne of God."*
7) Hebrews 2:10—*"For it was fitting for Him, for whom are all things, and through whom are all things, in bringing many sons to*

glory, to perfect the <u>author of their salvation</u> through sufferings."

As we saw in the New Covenant, God has the job of perfecting His children. He will not fail!

*For what does the
Scripture say?
"And Abraham believed
God, and it was reckoned
to him as righteousness."*
                Romans 4:3

Abraham's Conception
and Birth
Part Nine

⌗

In the last chapter we looked through a lot of
Scripture concerning those who are born again. In
this chapter and the next one, we will be studying
two very different men, Abraham and his grandson,
Jacob. Some of you may not like the title of these
two chapters. Yet most of us realize that *no* man is
ever born saved. No person comes into this world
as a Believer. I like talking to different people and
asking how God saved their souls. The stories will

just bless you. But some say, "Oh, I've always been a believer." Unfortunately, that's not possible! So it should not be a ridiculous stretch to think that the Bible might reveal <u>probable</u> spiritual landmarks in our forefathers' journey to God. Therefore, give me some time in the Word and let's see if it does give us some hint, when a spiritual conception and birth might have taken place in these men.

We will start with Abraham. The Bible calls him *"The father of all who believe"* (Romans 4:11) and, *"the friend of God"* (James 2:23). There is much we can gain from this man, as the Scriptures reveal some things we may not have heard or seen before.

Let's begin with Genesis 15:1-6, 18:

> *After these things <u>the word of the Lord came to Abram</u> in a vision, saying, "Do not fear, Abram, I am a shield to you; Your reward shall be very great." And Abram said, "O Lord God, what wilt Thou give me, since I am childless, and the heir of my house is Eliezer of Damascus?" And Abram said, "Since Thou hast given no offspring to me, one born in my house is my heir." Then behold, the word of the Lord came to him, saying, "This man will not be your heir; but one who shall come forth from your own body, he shall be your heir." And He took him outside and said, "Now look toward the heaven, and count the stars, if you are able to count them." And He said to him, "So shall your descendants be." <u>Then he</u>*

believed in the Lord; and He reckoned it to him as righteousness. On that day the Lord made a covenant with Abram, saying, "To your descendants I have given this land, from the river of Egypt as far as the great river, the river Euphrates."

Here is a list from the conversation between God and Abram:

- God comes to Abram in a vision (v. 1).
- God declares to Abram, *"I am a shield to you; your reward shall be very great"* (v. 1).
- Abram's concern: *"What wilt Thou give me, since I am childless"* (vss. 2-3).
- God confirms, *"But one who shall come forth from your own body, he shall be your heir"* (v. 4).
- God let Abram know that his descendants will be as the stars of heaven, unable to count them (v. 5).
- *Then he [Abram] believed in the Lord; and He reckoned it to him as righteousness* (v. 6).
- God makes a covenant with Abram (v. 18).

In verses 2-5 God assures Abram that he will have his own child. This is amazing because Abram is between seventy-five to eighty-five years old, and Sarai his wife ten years younger. Both of them are way past childbearing. God goes even further. He says that Abram's descendants will be so many that they cannot be counted.

Nevertheless, what I want us to really concentrate on is Abram's response. *"Then he believed in the Lord; and He [the Lord] reckoned it to him [Abram] as righteousness."* What do you think the Scripture means when it says, "He believed in the Lord"? To answer that we'll look at some passages in the New Testament that use this quote and see if it will shed some light.

1) Romans 4:1-8 —

What then shall we say that Abraham, our forefather according to the flesh, has found? For <u>if Abraham was justified by works</u>, he has something to boast about; but not before God. For what does the Scripture say? "<u>AND ABRAHAM BELIEVED GOD, AND IT WAS RECKONED TO HIM AS RIGHTEOUSNESS</u>." Now to the one who works, his wage is not reckoned as a favor, but as what is due. But to the one who does not work, <u>but believes in Him who justifies the ungodly,</u> his faith is reckoned as righteousness, just as David also speaks of the blessing upon the man to whom God reckons righteousness apart from works: "<u>Blessed are those whose lawless deeds have been forgiven,</u>And whose sins have been covered. Blessed is the man whose sin the Lord will not take into account."

The context here is, how ungodly men can become just before a holy God. It uses Abraham as the example. Verse 5, *"But to the one who does not work, but believes in Him who justifies the ungodly, HIS FAITH IS RECKONED AS RIGHTEOUS-NESS."* Abraham believed God could do the impossible and he recognized God as who He was, holy. I feel certain more was going on in Genesis 15 than we realize. I think it was more than Abram's desire for a son; he saw his lost condition, his ungodliness, and his desperate need for a savior. Remember, a savior was first promised in Genesis 3.

I want to bring something else to your attention. Notice in verses 2-5 that we are saved by faith not works. There are many religions that teach people to *do* work, good work, for their salvation. But no matter how much good you and I do, it will *never* buy us salvation. It has always been by faith. In fact, not only are we saved by faith, we are to live by faith. Romans 1:17b: *"But the righteous man shall live by faith."*

2) Galatians 3:6-9— *"Even so ABRAHAM BELIEVED GOD, AND IT WAS RECK-ONED TO HIM AS RIGHTEOUSNESS. Therefore, be sure that it is those who are of faith who are sons of Abraham. And the Scripture, foreseeing that God would justify the Gentiles by faith, preached the gospel beforehand to Abraham, saying, "All the nations shall be blessed in you." So then*

> ***<u>those who are of faith are blessed with
> Abraham, the believer</u>.***"

Let us review this Scripture:

- Again, we have this direct quote from Genesis 15:6, ***"Abraham believed God, and it was reckoned to him as righteousness."*** The context here is faith in God that saves a man's soul. ***"It is those who are of faith who are sons of Abraham."*** And, ***"foreseeing that God would justify the Gentiles by faith."***
- God ***"preached the gospel beforehand to Abraham [saying], 'All the nations shall be blessed in you.'"*** This verse is quoted from Genesis 12:3. Here the Scriptures tell us that God preached the gospel *beforehand* to Abraham. Let me say it again. God preached the gospel. Do you remember what the gospel is? The gospel is the good news that God has a savior for the world. It is therefore very likely that Abram had a spiritual conception sometime between leaving his home in Mesopotamia and Genesis 15.
- ***<u>So then those who are of faith are blessed with Abraham, the believer</u>.***" Abraham became a believer and I think that Scripture points to Genesis 15:6 as the time of his salvation.

Establishing this has significance, because if Abraham did not become a believer until Genesis 15, then those things he did beforehand show a man in search of God. A man who has Not obtain justification before God yet. What I'm trying to say is this. Scripture will reveal that Abraham heard God, and he (mostly) obeyed Him. He set up altars and he prayed to God. All of this and yet probably not a true believer! This can show that we can do religious duties and still not be born again.

Go with me to Genesis 11:31-32, *"And Terah took Abram his son, and Lot the son of Haran, his grandson, and Sarai his daughter-in-law, his son Abram's wife; and they went out together from Ur of the Chaldeans in order to enter the land of Canaan; and they went as far as Haran, and settled there. And the days of Terah were two hundred and five years; and Terah died in Haran.*

And now, Genesis 12:1-6:

<u>Now the Lord said to Abram, "Go forth from your country, and from your relatives and from your father's house, to the land which I will show you; and I will make you a great nation, and I will bless you, and make your name great; and so you shall be a blessing; and I will bless those who bless you,</u> and the one who curses you <u>I will curse. And in you all the families of the earth shall be blessed." So Abram went forth as the Lord had spoken to him; and Lot went with him.</u> Now Abram was seventy-five years old when he departed from Haran. And Abram took Sarai his wife and Lot his nephew, and all their possessions which they had accumulated, and the persons which they had acquired in Haran,

*and they set out for the land of Canaan;
thus they came to the land of Canaan. And
Abram passed through the land as far as the
site of Shechem, to the oak of Moreh. Now
the Canaanite was then in the land.*

Below is a list of the instructions and promises
God gave to Abram:

- God came to Abram (v. 1). Later, he gets his name changed to Abraham.
- God gave Abram instructions (v. 1).
  - o go forth from your country
  - o from your relatives
  - o from your father's house
  - o go to a land, which I will show you

- Then God made Abram some promises (vss. 2-3).
  - o I will make you a great nation
  - o I will bless you
  - o and make your name great
  - o and so you will be a blessing
  - o I will bless those that bless you
  - o and the one who curses you, I will curse
  - o and *in* you all the families of the earth will be blessed

Abram obeyed God (or did he fully?). He took
Lot (v. 4) and his father. Turn to Acts 7:1-4, so I can
explain. *"And the high priest said, 'Are these things
so?' And he said, 'Hear me, brethren and fathers!*

__The__ God of glory appeared to our father __Abraham__ __when he was in Mesopotamia, before he lived in__ __Haran__, and said to him, "__Depart from your country__ __and your relatives__, and come into the land that I will show you." Then he departed from the land of the Chaldeans, and settled in Haran. And from there, after his father died, God removed him into this country in which you are now living." This is Stephen speaking to the high priest before a group of people stoned him to death. He is giving some history of the Jewish people. In these verses we see that God actually came to Abram when he was in Mesopotamia. This was his home, the country he lived in be*f*ore he moved to Haran. God told him, *"Depart from your country __and your relatives__, and come into the land that I will show you."* Now you tell me. Did Abram leave his relatives behind? No! He took his father, Terah, and his nephew, Lot. So right from the start we see that he did not fully obey God. He took some relatives with him. Yes, he did leave town not knowing where he was going, but his obedience was not complete.

One thing that I do not want to escape our notice is that *God came to Abram.* We do not see Abram searching out God. *"There is none who seeks for God" (Romans 3:11b).* Also in our list, we see the promises God made to Abram. Here, like the New Covenant, we see God is going to do all that He promised. Repeatedly God says, "I WILL, I WILL, I WILL." Next, we see that Abram headed to the land of Canaan. Here God speaks to a man, gives him instructions and promises, and Abram obeys (mostly). Keep in mind that he was not yet a believer.

Let us keep reading. Genesis 12:7-9 says, "***And the Lord appeared to Abram and said, 'To your descendants I will give this land.' So he built an altar there to the Lord*** *who had appeared to him. Then he proceeded from there to the mountain on the east of Bethel, and pitched his tent, with Bethel on the west and Ai on the east; and there* ***he built an altar to the Lord and called upon the name of the Lord. And Abram journeyed on,*** *continuing toward the Negev."*

According to these verses:

- The Lord appeared a second time to Abram (v. 7).
- God makes him another promise (v. 7; to your descendants I will give this land).
- Abram builds an altar to the Lord (v. 7; this is the first time Scripture mentions him building an altar to the Lord, worship).
- Abram builds a second altar (v. 8) and calls on the name of the Lord. (The first time mentioned that Abram prays to God.)
- Abram continues on his journey (v. 9; he continues to obey God).

At this point, Abram has set up two altars. He is worshipping God and calling on His name. In Genesis 13:3-4, 18, we see a repeat of these actions. This is just astonishing to me; I was never taught that it is possible for an unregenerate, godless man to hear and obey God—let alone worship and pray to Him. This should speak volumes to us. I was taught that God would never hear a lost man's prayer, only the prayer for salvation. Yet, we've seen Scripture that a lost man talks with God.

It makes me remember what Jesus said in Matthew 7:21-23—*"Not everyone who says to Me [Jesus], 'Lord, Lord,' will enter the kingdom of heaven; <u>but he who DOES the will of My Father</u> who is in heaven. Many will say to Me on that day, 'Lord, Lord, did we not prophesy in Your name, and in Your name cast out demons, and in Your name perform many miracles?' And then I will declare to them, 'I NEVER KNEW YOU; depart from Me, <u>you who practice lawlessness.</u>'"* This is a frightful prospect. Here are some people who are dead, mind you, and they are standing before God at judgment. They seem confused. They seem convinced that they are true believers. *"Lord, Lord, did we not prophesy in Your name, and in Your name cast out demons, and in Your name perform many miracles?"* Yet they hear their end: *"I NEVER KNEW YOU; depart from Me, <u>you who practice lawlessness.</u>"* What about you? I beg you to be sure!

Before we close I would like to address the issue of eternal salvation. I know that there are many of you out there who believe a person can be truly saved and then fall away, that they can lose their salvation. In fact, people use that to explain much of the Scripture that we have covered so far. You must get this vital issue settled. Ask yourself why you believe that, and then begin to search the Scriptures to know for sure. Jesus could not say, ***"Truly, truly, I say to you, he who believes has eternal life" (John 6:47)*** if we could lose it. If that were the case, He would have said, "Truly, truly, I say to you, he who believes has temporary life." But He did not. Once Jesus saves you, you are truly saved. You can never lose it. The problem is that for many people, they were not saved in the first place!

He has remembered His covenant for ever, the word which He commanded to a thousand generations.
Psalm 105:8

Jacob, His Conception and Birth
Part Ten

As we searched the Scriptures concerning Abraham in the previous section we found that he obeyed, prayed, and worshipped God, although he was not yet saved. Here I would like us to look at Jacob and see if we can discover the possible time of his spiritual conception and birth.

Go with me to Genesis 27 and 28. Jacob has deceived Isaac, his father, out of Esau's (his brother) blessing. Esau swore to kill him (Genesis 27:41), so Jacob's mom sends him to her relative's house in Paddan-aram (Genesis 28:2).

We'll pick up the story in Genesis 28:10-22:

Then Jacob departed from Beersheba and went toward Haran. And he came to a certain place and spent the night there, because the sun had set; and he took one of the stones of the place and put it under his head, and lay down in that place. And he had a dream, and behold, a ladder was set on the earth with its top reaching to heaven; and behold, the angels of God were ascending and descending on it. And behold, the Lord stood above it and said, "I am the Lord, the God of your father Abraham and the God of Isaac; the land on which you lie, I will give it to you and to your descendants. Your descendants shall also be like the dust of the earth, and you shall spread out to the west and to the east and to the north and to the south; and in you and in your descendants shall all the families of the earth be blessed. And behold, I am with you, and will keep you wherever you go, and will bring you back to this land; for I will not leave you until I have done what I have promised you." Then Jacob awoke from his sleep and said, "Surely the Lord is in this place, and I did not know it." And he was afraid and said, "How awesome is this place! This is none other than the house of God, and this is the gate of heaven." So Jacob rose early in the morning, and took the stone that he had put *under his head and set it up as a pillar, and poured oil on its top. And he called the name of that place Bethel; however, previously the name of the city had been Luz. Then <u>Jacob made a vow, saying, "If God will be with me</u> and will keep me on this journey that I take, and will give me food to eat and garments to wear, and I return to my father's house in safety, <u>then the Lord will be my God.</u>*

Let us make a list of this event:

- God came to Jacob in a dream (v. 12). Again God makes the first move.
- God introduces Himself: "I am the Lord, the God of your father Abraham and the God of Isaac." It is interesting God does not say I'm your God too (v. 13).
- God confirms the covenant He made with Abraham (Genesis 12, 13, 15, 17) and Isaac (Genesis 26:1-5), and extends it to Jacob:
  - o The land on which you lie, I will give it to you and to your descendants.
  - o Your descendants shall also be like the dust of the earth, and you shall spread out to the west and to the east and to the north and to the south.
  - o And in you and in your descendants shall all the families of the earth be blessed (vss. 13-14). Remember this from Abraham (Genesis 12:3; Galatians 3:8).

- We can assume that God also preached the gospel to Jacob here.
- God makes some personal promises to Jacob:
    - o Behold I am with you,
    - o and will keep you wherever you go,
    - o and will bring you back to this land
    - o for I will not leave you until I have done what I have promised you (vs.15).

- Jacob awoke and acknowledges, *"How awesome is this place! This is none other than the house of God, and this is the gate of heaven"* (vs. 16).
- Jacob sets up a pillar as a memorial (vs. 18).
- Jacob makes a vow (vs. 20-21).

Again, we see that God came to man first. Jacob is not found seeking God. God sought him out and made these promises to him. We must remember what we saw in Romans 3:11, *"There is none who understands, there is none who seeks for God."* Man does not seek God, but it is God who reveals Himself to man *first*. We must also remember that Jacob is the grandson of Abraham. He has heard all the stories of how God called Abraham out of his homeland, gave him the promises, and made a covenant with him. God had come to Jacob's father Isaac in Genesis 26:1-5 and confirmed this same covenant with him. Therefore, we know that Jacob had to have had some kind of belief in God. Look at his response when he woke up. Genesis 28:16-19—*"Then Jacob awoke from his sleep and said, 'Surely the Lord is in this place, and I did not know it.' And he was afraid and said, 'How awesome is this place! This is none other than the house of God, and this is the gate of heaven.' So Jacob rose early in the morning, and took the stone that he had put under his head and set it up as a pillar, and poured oil on its top. And he called the name of that place Bethel; however, previously the name of the city had been Luz."* All of this sounds like a man who believes in the Lord. In fact, the name Jacob called that place is Bethel, which means the house of God. Would you say that Jacob is a believer? Saved? Well, we'll see.

Now let us look at the vow Jacob made. Genesis 28:20-22 — *"Then Jacob made a vow, saying, 'If God will be with me and will keep me on this journey that I take, and will give me food to eat and garments to wear, and I return to my father's house in safety, THEN the Lord will be my God. And this stone, which I have set up as a pillar, will be God's house; and of all that Thou dost give me I will surely give a tenth to Thee.'"* Do you see what the Scriptures reveal? Jacob is saying, "**IF God will keep His word to me (Genesis 28:15)** and keep me on this journey, and make sure I have plenty of food and clothing, and I return to my father's house safely, **THEN** the Lord will be **MY** God!" I don't know about you, but this is just amazing! Here is a man who has just had a supernatural encounter with the living God. God has established the covenant He made with his father and grandfather, and even gave him some personal promises. Yet, Jacob has decided to wait and see if

God does what He says and *if* He does come through, *THEN he will make the Lord his God.*

The Scriptures answered our question. Was Jacob saved at this time? *No*, he was not saved. Though he did have some of belief in God, it was not to the saving of his soul. The only thing that has taken place here is possibly a spiritual conception. Jacob is not choosing the Lord as his God, at least not yet. Is all of this a revelation for you? I hope so. For much too long we have believed what others have taught us; to *our shame,* we are discovering that some of it is just *not truth*!

From the first time Scripture mentions Jacob in Genesis 25:19 through to chapter 31, you will find many interesting facts, some of which were different than Abraham's. These passages show a deceitful, self-centered man. Nowhere in all of those chapters will you find that Jacob ever set up an altar or prayed to God. In fact, not until Genesis 32 do we find him praying and seeking God, and this was on his way back home, twenty years later. Like Abraham though, God sought Jacob.

Now let's finish the story. In Genesis 32, Jacob is headed home. He is very concerned that Esau has not forgotten what he did to him when he left. Therefore, Jacob is afraid for his family's safety, and his own. In desperation, we find for the first time Jacob is praying to God. Read with me, if you will, his prayer in Genesis 32:9-12:

And Jacob said, <u>"O God of my father Abraham and God of my father Isaac, O</u>

Lord, who didst say to me, 'Return to your country and to your relatives, and I will prosper you,' <u>**I am unworthy of all the loving kindness and of all the faithfulness which Thou hast shown**</u> **to Thy servant; for with my staff only I crossed this Jordan, and now I have become two companies. Deliver me, I pray, from the hand of my brother, from the hand of Esau; for I fear him, lest he come and attack me, the mothers with the children.** <u>**For Thou didst say, 'I will surely prosper you, and make your descendants as the sand of the sea, which cannot be numbered for multitude.**</u>**'"**

Do you see it in verse nine? Jacob is praying to the *God of his father Abraham* and the *God of his father Isaac*. Jacob still has not made God *his* God! Can you believe this? Twenty years have gone by according to Genesis 31:38 since Jacob had his first encounter with God, and Jacob still has not made the Lord his God.

In his first prayer, we find Jacob a very humble man, in a most distressed state. Jacob acknowledges that it was God's loving-kindness and faithfulness that brought about all his blessings. Jacob is also reminding God of the promises He previously made to him. It is amazing that within a twenty-year span, Jacob has not forgotten these. Even though he has not made Him his God yet, we find Jacob begging God to deliver him from Esau.

The night before Jacob and Esau are to meet, Jacob sends all of his belongings and his family across the brook of Jabbok. Read with me this most memorial event in Jacob's life in Genesis 32:24-31:

Then Jacob was left alone, and <u>a man wrestled with him until daybreak</u>. And when he saw that he had not prevailed against him, he touched the socket of his thigh; so the socket of Jacob's thigh was dislocated while he wrestled with him. Then he said, "Let me go, for the dawn is breaking." But he said, <u>"I will not let you go unless you bless me</u>." So he said to him, "What is your name?" And he said, "Jacob." And he said, "Your name shall no longer be Jacob, but Israel; for <u>you have striven with God and with men and have prevailed</u>." Then Jacob asked him and said, "Please tell me your name." But he said, "Why is it that you ask my name?" And <u>he blessed him there</u>. So Jacob named the place Peniel, for he said, <u>"I have seen God face to face</u>, yet my life has been preserved." Now the sun rose upon him just as he crossed over Penuel, and he was limping on his thigh.

We do not want to miss a thing, so let us make our list:

- Jacob wrestles with a man (v. 24; Hosea 12:2-5 says it was an angel).

170

- They wrestle all night long (vss. 22, 26).

- Jacob refuses to turn loose of the angel until he blesses him (v. 26).

- Jacob gets a name change. ***"Your name shall no longer be Jacob, but Israel; for you have striven with God and with men and have prevailed"*** (vss. 27-28). The name Jacob means a *deceiver*. The name Israel means *prince of God*. These two definitions imply more than just a name change, possibly a heart change.

- ***"For you have striven with God and with men and have prevailed"*** (v. 28). The meaning of the word *striven* is to have power like a prince. Therefore, between Jacob's name being changed to *prince of God*, and the word *striven*, stating that he has *power like a prince* we can again note that much has taken place within Jacob. All of Jacob's life he had schemed and manipulated situations to get his way. Now we begin to see a change.

- The angel blesses Jacob (v. 29). What could the blessing have been? Was it a financial blessing? No, Jacob already had that (Genesis 31:1 and 32:10). Was it just the assurance of safety from his brother Esau? I am sure this was a part of the blessing, but somehow I am convinced it was much more than that.

- Jacob names the place Peniel for he said, ***"I have seen God face to face"*** (v. 30). The definition of the word *Peniel* is the *face of God*.

- ***"I have seen God face to face, yet my life has been preserved"*** (v. 30). The word for *life* in this verse actually means *breath* or *soul*. This verse is not talking about the physical body, but the soul of man. In addition, the word *preserved* means *to deliver*. So you tell me; what could Jacob's soul been delivered from?

In Genesis 33:1-4, we find Jacob meets Esau. Esau is not mad at Jacob, and he is actually glad to see him. As the chapter progresses we find Jacob bringing his whole family into Canaan and settling them in the city of Shechem. Genesis 33:17-20— *"And Jacob journeyed to Succoth; and built for himself a house, and made booths for his livestock, therefore the place is named Succoth. Now Jacob came safely to the city of Shechem, which is in the land of Canaan, when he came from Paddan-aram, and camped before the city. And he bought the piece of land where he had pitched his tent from the hand of the sons of Hamor, Shechem's father, for one hundred pieces of money. <u>Then he erected there an altar, and called it El-Elohe-Israel.</u>"*

Jacob is back in the land of promise, Canaan. He builds a house for his family and settles down. Read verse twenty with me. *"Then he erected there an altar, and called it El-Elohe-Israel."* Here is the first time that Jacob builds an altar to the Lord. Not only did he build an altar but look what he called it, *El-Elohe-Israel*, which means, *God, the God of Israel!* Remember he got his name changed to Israel. For the *first time* Jacob/Israel is declaring that *God is his God!*

Look what happened after this. Genesis 35:1-4:

Then God said to Jacob, "Arise, go up to Bethel, and live there; and make an altar there to God, who appeared to you when you fled from your brother Esau." So Jacob said to his household and to all who were with him, "Put away the foreign gods which are among you, and purify yourselves, and change your garments; and let us arise and go up to Bethel; and I will make an altar there to God, who answered me in the day of my distress, and has been with me wherever I have gone." So they gave to Jacob all the foreign gods which they had, and the rings which were in their ears; and Jacob hid them under the oak which was near Shechem.

Do you see how Jacob is beginning to live? For a long time, he has allowed false gods in his home. Jacob seems like a changed man. He no longer deceives and schemes but puts his trust in God. He is even taking responsibility for his family's spiritual well being: *"So Jacob said to his household and to all who were with him, 'Put away the foreign gods which are among you, and purify yourselves, and change your garments.'"*

I believe it's possible that Jacob had a spiritual conception when God first spoke to him in Genesis 28:12-22. Nevertheless, somewhere between then and Jacob wrestling with the angel in Genesis 32:24-32, a spiritual conception took place. But it's at Penuel, where Jacob wrestles with the angel, that I think he became a believer like Abraham. It is from this point that we begin to see evidence of a changed life.

If you continue to read the rest of Jacob's story you will find that he lived the remainder of his days walking according to God's commands. No, he was not perfect, but he was a new man. Jacob had finally *made the Lord his God!*

Now let us review both Abraham and Jacob, two very different men. Abraham had a spiritual conception somewhere between God first calling him, until he truly became born again. Remember he was worshipping, praying, hearing, and even obeying God. However, his salvation didn't take place until Genesis 15. Jacob, on the other hand, had a spiritual conception as well (Genesis 28), but we do not find him setting up altars nor praying of any kind; yet both were lost.

After their salvation, you will discover that both of their lives proved that they were children of God. Their lives declared to all the heathen nations around them that God was with them. He was now their God.

What proof is in your life that you are a Believer? Keep in mind there is a difference between being good and being godly. Godliness comes *only from God*. Man cannot produce it. So are you godly or just good? Have you become a *new creature in Christ*? Nothing short of this will keep your soul from hell!

You believe that
God is one.
You do well;
the demons also believe and
shudder.

James 2:19

Faith Without Works Is Dead!
Part Eleven

S o far we've read that there's more to *just believe* than we realized. Now we're going to look at some people in the Bible of whom the Scriptures say, *they believed.* We'll observe the context closely and make some lists. After examining the evidence we'll see if they could be convicted in a court of law for being a follower of Jesus Christ. If so, then their faith was genuine. If not, whatever kind of faith they had, it was not the saving kind.

Since we are going to be observing a passage from the gospel of John, we should find the author's reason for writing this book. Let's go to John 20:30-31—*"Many other signs therefore Jesus also performed in the presence of the disciples, which are not written in this book; but these have been written that you may believe that Jesus is the Christ, the Son of God; and that believing you may have life in His name."* The author of John has shared many events where Jesus performed miracles. He used these signs to prove to his readers that Jesus is the Christ, the Son of God, in hope that they would believe and accept Him for themselves.

In chapter eight of John, we find Jesus having different conversations with diverse groups as He was teaching in the temple. We are going to turn our attention to a certain group of Jews. We will begin our reading in John 8:30-32—*"As He spoke these things, many came to believe in Him. Jesus therefore was saying to those Jews who had believed Him, "IF you abide in My word, then you are truly disciples of Mine; and you shall know the truth, and the truth shall make you free."* This is wonderful! Jesus was teaching in the temple and these Jews came to believe in Him. Does this sound as if they are Christians? It does to me, but before we get too excited, let's examine the conversation that Jesus had with these Jews who had believed Him.

This passage is too important to pass up. It has a very small word *if* that is significant. This is a conditional particle, meaning that part B is true *only if* part A is true. For example:

IF_____(A)_____THEN_____(B)_____

Now fill in the blanks.

IF ***If you abide in My word*** THEN ***you are truly disciples of Mine***.

Let's look at three words in this verse.

1) The word, *abide* means *to remain* or *to stay in one place*.
2) The word *truly* means *the real thing*.
3) The word for *disciple* means *a learner* or *a student*. It does not mean that this learner is a child of God.

Jesus warns that these Jews who believed in Him could be exposed as false disciples *if* they did not remain in His word. Somehow, we've been taught that whenever we see the word *disciple* in the Bible, it automatically means a Christian. That is *not true!* Look at what 2 Corinthians 11:13-15 has to say: ***"For such men are false apostles, deceitful workers, disguising themselves as apostles of Christ. And no wonder, for even Satan disguises himself as an angel of light. Therefore it is not surprising if his servants also disguise themselves as servants of righteousness; whose end shall be according to their deeds."*** There are false apostles, disciples, teachers, and prophets. So beware! Notice that their end shall be according to their DEEDS!

Now let's read the whole conversation Jesus had with these Jews who believed in Him. John 8:30-47 —

As He spoke these things, <u>many came to believe in Him.</u> Jesus therefore was saying to those Jews who had believed Him, "If you abide in My word, then you are truly disciples of Mine; and you shall know the truth, and the truth shall make you free." They answered Him, <u>"We are Abraham's offspring</u>, and have never yet been enslaved to anyone; [This is not true; Abraham's offspring had been enslaved many times: in Egypt, in the Book of Judges, etc.] *how is it that You say, 'You shall become free'?" Jesus answered them, "Truly, truly, I say to you, everyone who commits sin is the slave of sin. And the slave does not remain in the house forever; the son does remain forever.* [Jesus is explaining that the freedom He is speaking about is freedom from sin. Remember Romans 6?] *If therefore the Son shall make you free, you shall be free indeed. I know that you are Abraham's offspring; yet <u>you seek to kill Me, because My word has no place in you.</u> I speak the things which I have seen with My Father; therefore you also do the things which you heard from <u>your father.</u>" They answered and said to Him, "Abraham is our father." Jesus said to them, "If you are Abraham's*

178

children, do the deeds of Abraham. But as it is, you are <u>seeking to kill Me</u>, a man who has told you the truth, which I heard from God; this Abraham did not do. You are doing the <u>deeds of your father.</u>" They said to Him, "We were not born of fornication; we have one Father, even God." Jesus said to them, "<u>If God were your Father, you would love Me</u>; for I proceeded forth and have come from God, for I have not even come on My own initiative, but He sent Me. Why do <u>you not understand what I am saying? It is because you cannot hear My word. You are of your father the devil,</u> and you want to do the desires of your father. He was a murderer from the beginning, and does not stand in the truth, because there is no truth in him. Whenever he speaks a lie, he speaks from his own nature; for he is a liar, and the father of lies. But <u>because I speak the truth, you do not believe Me</u>. Which one of you convicts Me of sin? If <u>I speak truth, why do you not believe Me? He who is of God hears the words of God</u>; for this reason <u>you do not hear them, because you are not of God</u>."

Let us compile a chart regarding *how the Scripture describes* these Jews that believed Him.

- They were Abraham's offspring (vss. 33, 37).
- They sought to kill Jesus because (vss. 37, 40).

- His word had no place in them (v. 37).
- They did the things which they heard from [their] father (v. 38).
- They confessed, "Abraham is our father" (v. 39).
- Jesus said, *"If you are Abraham's children, do the deeds of Abraham"* (v. 39).
- They were doing the deeds of their father (vss. 38, 41).
- They confessed that they *"had one Father, even God"* (v. 41).
- Jesus said to them, *"If God were your Father, you would love Me"* (v. 42).
- They did not understand what Jesus was saying, because they could not hear Jesus' words. (v. 43).
- They were of their father the devil (v. 44).
- They wanted to do the desires of their father the devil (kill, lie; v. 44).
- Because Jesus spoke the truth, they did not believe Him (v. 45).
- Jesus was speaking the truth, but they did not believe Him (v. 46).
- Jesus said, *"He who is of God hears the words of God; for this reason <u>you do not hear [them] because you are not of God</u>."* They did not hear God's words, because they were not of God (v. 47).

Does this surprise you? Would you have put this list together with people who believed in Jesus? Regardless of what you thought, it's right there in the

Bible. Jesus really exposes what kind of belief they had. What do you think they believed? Maybe they believed facts about Jesus. It is possible that they even believed that He was truly the Son of God, the Christ. The Bible does not tell us, but from Jesus' description, He uncovered them to be false believers and false disciples. Their belief had not reached a point that produced salvation. Maybe they believed, but were not willing to surrender their life to Jesus. Whatever the explanation, it is clear; Jesus said, "*You are not of God*" (v. 46) and "*your father is the devil*" (v. 44).

Turn with me to Acts 8:9-24, another Scripture that mentions a man who believed.

Now there was a certain <u>man named Simon, who formerly was practicing magic</u> in the city, and astonishing the people of Samaria, claiming to be someone great; and they all, from smallest to greatest, were giving attention to him, saying, <u>"This man is what is called the Great Power of God.</u>" And they were giving him attention because he had for a long time astonished them with his magic arts. But when they believed Philip preaching the good news about the kingdom of God and the name of Jesus Christ, they were being baptized, men and women alike. And even Simon himself believed; and after being baptized, he continued on with Philip; and as he observed signs and great miracles taking place, he was constantly amazed.

Now when the apostles in Jerusalem heard that Samaria had received the word of God, they sent them Peter and John, who came down and prayed for them, that they might receive the Holy Spirit. For He had not yet fallen upon any of them; they had simply been baptized in the name of the Lord Jesus. <u>Then they began laying their hands on them, and they were receiving the Holy Spirit.</u> Now when Simon saw that the Spirit was bestowed through the laying on of the apostles' hands, he offered them money, saying, "<u>Give this authority to me as well, so that everyone on whom I lay my hands may receive the Holy Spirit.</u>" But Peter said to him, "May your silver <u>perish</u> with you, because you thought you could obtain the gift of God with money! You have <u>no part or portion</u> in this matter, for your heart is not right before God. Therefore repent of this <u>wickedness</u> of yours, and pray the Lord that if possible, the intention of your heart may be forgiven you. For I see that you are in the <u>gall of bitterness</u> and in the <u>bondage of iniquity.</u>" But Simon answered and said, "Pray to the Lord for me yourselves, so that nothing of what you have said may come upon me." And so, when they had solemnly testified and spoken the word of the Lord, they started back to Jerusalem, and were preaching the gospel to many villages of the Samaritans.

Here is our list of Simon:

- Simon formerly was practicing magic (v. 9).
- He had astonished the people of Samaria, claiming to be someone great (v. 9).
- People had been saying this about Simon, "This man is what is called the Great Power of God" (v. 10).
- Then Philip came and the people believed his preaching of the good news about the kingdom of God and the name of Jesus Christ, and they were being baptized, men and women alike (v. 12).
- Simon himself believed (v. 13).
- Simon was baptized, and he continued with Philip (v. 13).
- Simon observed signs and great miracles taking place, and was amazed (v. 13).
- Peter and John came down and prayed for the people, that they might receive the Holy Spirit. (vss. 14-16).
- Peter and John [began] laying their hands on them, and they were receiving the Holy Spirit (v. 17).
- When Simon saw that the Spirit was bestowed through the laying on of the apostles' hands, he offered them money (v. 18).
- Simon said, "Give this authority to me as well, so that everyone on whom I lay my hands may receive the Holy Spirit" (v. 19).
- But Peter said to him, "May your silver **perish with you**, because you thought you could

obtain the gift of God with money! (v. 20). In this verse, we see that it was not just Simon's silver that would perish but himself also. The definition of *perish* is *utter destruction, ruin,* and *perdition.* In the context, the implication is total ruin, which is much more than a physical death; it's total damnation.

- Peter said to Simon, "You have no part or portion in this matter, for your heart is not right before God" (v. 21). It is interesting to note, that we're not told that Simon received the Holy Spirit. Peter also exposes Simon's heart; it's not right with God.

- Peter continued speaking to Simon, "Therefore *repent of this wickedness* of yours" (v. 22). This word *repent* is the same word that both Jesus and John the Baptist used in the following passages—Mark 1:15, *"The time is fulfilled, and the kingdom of God is at hand; <u>repent and believe in the gospel</u>."* and, Matthew 3:2: *"<u>Repent</u>, for the kingdom of heaven is at hand."*

- Peter said, "Pray the Lord that if possible, the *intention of your heart* may be forgiven you" (v. 22). Please understand that salvation is a heart issue!

- Peter said, "For I see that you are in the **gall of bitterness**" (v. 23). This "gall of bitterness" stands for extreme wickedness, a product of evil fruit. Peter told Simon, "You are in the bondage of iniquity" (v. 23). Meaning that Simon is still a slave to sin. Remember what

Jesus told the "Jews that believed Him" in John 8:34-36? ***"Jesus answered them, 'Truly, truly, I say to you, <u>everyone who commits sin is the slave of sin</u>. And the slave does not remain in the house forever; the son does remain forever. If therefore the Son shall make you free, you shall be free indeed.'"*** Simon is not free! He is not saved!

- Simon answered and said, "*Pray to the Lord for me yourselves*, so that nothing of what you have said may come upon me" (v. 24). Notice Simon does not pray *for_himself*, but asks that Peter pray for him. A man must pray and repent to God for himself.

This is the only time that this man Simon is mentioned in the Bible. All we know about him is what we have right here. From these passages and the definitions of some of these words, it does not seem likely that he was a true believer. Yet Acts 8:13 says, ***"And even Simon himself believed; and after being baptized, he continued on with Philip."***

So here we have another Scripture that seems to shed doubt about a man's salvation experience. The Bible can say a person believes and not be a true believer. That is why it is of utmost importance that we keep Scripture in the context is it found. We also must not add to Scripture so that we can "feel" better about what it says. We must let Scripture speak for itself!

In the passage about Simon, we are reminded again that a person can make a profession to know

Jesus, and yet not possess Jesus or eternal life. Scripture tells us that, Simon had extreme wickedness in his life and he was in the bondage to iniquity (Acts 8:23). This reaffirms that how a person lives reveals if he has truly accepted Jesus as Savior and Lord.

What about you, do you believe? How do you live? If you are not sure about your salvation I can promise you one thing, God tells us in Jeremiah 29:13, *"And you will seek Me and find Me, when you search for Me with all your heart."* We should NEVER stop searching after God. *"For God is not a man that He should lie" (Numbers 23:19).* We can trust in His promises! If you are not saved, keep seeking after God and His truth, and you SHALL find Him! I want to remind you, that if you are seeking God, it is *only* because His love and mercy is drawing you to seek Him, John 6:44. So don't take it for granted.

Some of you are saying, "She is making salvation to be hard, and it's simple." Well, when I read Scripture it does not sound like salvation is simple. Matthew 7:13-14 says, *"Enter by the narrow gate; for the gate is wide, and <u>the way is broad that leads to destruction, and many are those who enter by it. For the gate is small, and the way is narrow that leads to life, and few are those who find it</u>."* According to Scripture, not many people find the way to eternal life. In this verse, it says few. The meaning of the word *few* is *puny in number*. That does not sound very simple to me, and the crowds aren't headed that way.

Look at Luke 13:23-24—*"And someone said to Him, 'Lord, are there just a few who are being saved?' And He said to them, 'Strive to enter by the narrow door; for many, I tell you, will seek to enter and will not be able.'"* This is truly heartbreaking, yet our Lord said it. Many will seek to enter and will not be able. Why? I don't know all the answers, maybe you should ask God!

I am concerned that in our culture we have taken grace and have done what Jude 3 says, *"Beloved, while I was making every effort to write you about our common salvation, I felt the necessity to write to you appealing that you contend earnestly for the faith which was once for all delivered to the saints. For certain persons have crept in unnoticed, those who were long beforehand marked out for this condemnation, ungodly persons who turn the grace of our God into licentiousness and deny our only Master and Lord, Jesus Christ."* Jude was very concerned about "these certain persons." They crept into the church unnoticed. Do you see what Jude tells us they did? These are *"Ungodly persons who turn the grace of our God into licentiousness and deny our only Master and Lord, Jesus Christ."* They turned the GRACE of God into licentiousness. The word *licentiousness* means *no restraints*, to live any way you want to, if it feels good do it! That sure sounds like our culture today.

Listen to what else Jude said about these certain persons. They *"deny our only Master and Lord, Jesus Christ."* Now think this through with me. Could someone sneak into the church and verbally

187

deny Christ as being Lord and Savior and be unnoticed? I think NOT! What happened is that these "certain persons" professed to KNOW Christ. They claimed to be Christians and because they made a so-called profession, the rest of the church did not question their salvation. But Jude said they *"denied our only Master and Lord Jesus Christ."* How did they DENY Jesus? They denied Him by the way they lived—licentious, no restraints!

We have allowed grace to become a license to sin. There is much more depth to the grace of God than what we have been taught. The grace that God gives to man is what enables him to live a righteous life, not an excuse to live a life of "licentiousness". Here is the list from Jude describing these certain persons. Look at it very carefully and you decide if they are Christians or not.

Jude

- A. For certain persons have crept in unnoticed (v. 4).
- B. Those who were long before marked out for this condemnation (v. 4).
- C. Ungodly persons who turn the grace of God into licentiousness (v. 4).
- D. And deny our only Master and Lord Jesus Christ (v. 4).
- E. These men revile the things which they do not understand (v. 10).

F. The things which they know by instinct, like unreasoning animals, by these things they are destroyed (v. 10).

G. Woe to them! For they have gone the way of Cain (v. 11).

H. For pay they have rushed headlong into the error of Balaam (v. 11).

I. They perished in the rebellion of Korah (v. 11).

J. These men are those who are hidden reefs in your love feast (v. 12).

K. They feast with you without fear, caring for themselves (v. 12).

L. Clouds without water, carried along by winds (v. 12).

M. Autumn trees without fruit (v. 12).

N. Doubly dead, uprooted (v. 12).

O. Wild waves of the sea, casting up their own shame like foam (v. 13).

P. Wandering stars for whom the black darkness has been reserved forever (v. 13).

Q. About these Enoch prophesied, ***"Behold, the Lord came with many thousands of His holy ones, to execute judgment upon all, and to convict all the ungodly of all their ungodly deeds which they have done in an ungodly way, and of all the harsh things which ungodly sinners have spoken against Him."*** (vss. 14-15).

R. These are grumblers, finding fault (v. 16).

S. Following after their own lust (v. 16).

T. They speak arrogantly, flattering people for the sake of gaining an advantage (v. 16).

U. Mockers (v. 18).

V. Following after their own ungodly lust (v. 18).

W. These are the ones who cause divisions (v. 19).

X. Worldly minded (v. 19).

Y. Devoid of the Spirit (v. 19).

You will also find this same truth in 2 Peter 2:1-3—*"But false prophets also arose among the people, just as there will also be false teachers among you, <u>who will secretly introduce destructive heresies, even denying the Master</u> who bought them, bringing swift destruction upon themselves. And many will follow their sensuality, and because of them <u>the way of the truth will be maligned;</u> and in their greed they will exploit you with false words; their judgment from long ago is not idle, and their destruction is not asleep."*

Here's our list:

- False prophets, false teachers, who will secretly introduce destructive heresies (v. 1),
- denying the Master (Jesus).
- Bringing swift destruction upon themselves (v. 1)
- Many will follow their sensuality (ruin) (v. 2)
- Because of them the way of the truth will be maligned; blasphemed (v. 2).

- In their greed they will exploit you with false words (v. 3).
- Their judgment from long ago is not idle, and their destruction (spiritual ruin) is not asleep.

This is not a list I would want to be associated with. This description is of a lost man. Let's look at one more Scripture. Turn to Titus 1:10-16:

For there are many rebellious men, empty talkers and deceivers, especially those of the circumcision, who must be silenced because they are upsetting whole families, teaching things they should not teach, for the sake of sordid gain. One of themselves, a prophet of their own, said, "Cretans are always liars, evil beasts, lazy gluttons." This testimony is true. For this cause reprove them severely that they may be sound in the faith, not paying attention to Jewish myths and commandments of men who turn away from the truth. To the pure, all things are pure; but to those who are defiled and unbelieving, nothing is pure, but both their mind and their conscience are defiled. They profess to know God, but by their deeds they deny Him, being detestable and disobedient, and worthless for any good deed.

Also see Titus 3:10-11—*"Reject a factious man after the first and second warning, knowing that such a man is perverted and is sinning, being self-condemned."*

Let's make a list:

- there are many rebellious men
- empty talkers
- deceivers
- especially those of the circumcision
- who must be silenced because they are upsetting (overthrowing the faith of someone, whole families) teaching things they should not teach for the sake of sordid gain
- one of them, a prophet of their own, said, "Cretans are always liars, evil beasts, and lazy gluttons."
- for this cause reprove them severely that they may be sound in the faith
- men who turn away from the truth
- but to those who are defiled and unbelieving (lost, without God) nothing is pure
- but both their mind and their conscience are defiled
- *they profess to know God, but by their deeds they deny Him*
- being detestable and disobedient
- worthless for any good deed
- perverted
- sinning
- self-condemned

These last three Scripture references have a lot in common. One, those who were causing the problems were, *in the church!* They all had professed to know Jesus, but the message they were spreading was a twisted gospel, not the truth. Paul says in Galatians 1:6-8, *"I am amazed that you are so quickly deserting Him who called you by the grace of Christ, for a different gospel; which is really not another; only there are some who are disturbing you, and want to distort the Gospel of Christ. But even though we, or an angel from heaven, should preach to you a gospel contrary to that which we have preached to you, let him be accursed."* This has gone on from the beginning of time. Satan has always tried to both pervert and twist God's words.

> The true gospel is this: *"For I delivered to you as of first importance what I also received, that Christ died for our sins according to the Scriptures, and that He was buried, and that He was raised on the third day according to the Scriptures"*
>
> *(1 Corinthians 15:3-4).*

Another thing that Jude, 2 Peter 2:1-3, and Titus 1:10-16 have in common is that these people all denied Jesus Christ by the way they lived, and their end is clear—eternal damnation!

Last, they were trying to lead others away from Jesus and His truth, proclaiming that you can have faith and believe in Jesus and yet live however you choose. But Scripture declares that the proof of *real* faith and genuine belief in Jesus Christ is shown when we seek Him and His will, and obey His commands. When this happens you will live a righteous life.

Go to one more Scripture to seal this thought, James 2:14-24:

> *What use is it, my brethren, <u>if a man SAYS he has faith, but he has NO WORKS? Can that faith save him?</u> If a brother or sister is without clothing and in need of daily food, and one of you says to them, "Go in peace, be warmed and be filled," and yet you do not give them what is necessary for their body, what use is that? <u>Even so faith, if it has no works, is dead, being by itself.</u> But someone may well say, "You have faith, and I have works; show me your faith without works, and I will show you my faith by my works. <u>You believe God is one. You do well; the demons also believe, and shudder.</u> But are you willing to recognize, you foolish fellow, <u>that faith without works is useless?</u> Was not Abraham our father justified by works, when he offered up Isaac his son on the altar? You see that faith was working with his works, and as a result of the works, faith was perfected. And the <u>Scripture was fulfilled</u> which says, "And Abraham believed God and it was reckoned to Him as righteousness," and he was called a friend of God. You see that a man is justified by works, and not faith alone.*

A lot of people have a problem with James. It seems as if he is saying that we must work for our salvation, but remember Romans 4:4-5 told us, *"Now to the one who works, his wage is not reckoned as a favor, but as what is due. But to the one who does not work, <u>but believes in Him who justifies the ungodly, his faith is reckoned as righteousness</u>."* James is agreeing with this Scripture as well as Ephesians 2:8-9: *"For by grace are you have been saved through faith; and that not of yourselves, it is a gift of God; not as a result of works, that no one should boast."* James is giving us a little more. He is saying: we can't work for our salvation, but when we are truly saved, the good works *prove* our salvation.

For God so loved the world,
that He gave His only
begotten Son,
that whosoever believes in
Him should not perish,
but have eternal life.
John 3:16

Judas and Hebrews Six
Part Twelve

I n this chapter, I would like to show how very near to Jesus a person can come and yet fall short of salvation. How a person can walk with Jesus, have many spiritual gifts, and even be effective for God, yet like Matthew Mead said, "Be but almost a Christian." Judas Iscariot is the prime example of this. He was one of Jesus' twelve hand-picked apostles. He was with Christ from the beginning of His ministry. He walked, talked, ate, and ministered with Jesus and the other eleven. In the end he fell away.

It's interesting that many people just assumed he was saved. It's hopeful thinking, that when we all die that everyone goes to heaven, except for the really bad people. Unfortunately, that's not true. Many of us would rather believe a lie because it feels better than the truth. Nevertheless, I hope to encourage you to see and desire truth so you are not deceived.

We'll look at Scripture and examine how it describes Judas Iscariot. By now you know the routine; we'll make some lists and see what conclusions we can come to.

Here we go! Let's start!

1) Luke 6:12-17—*And it was at this time that He [Jesus] went off to the mountain to pray, and He spent the whole night in prayer to God. And when day came, He called His disciples to Him; and chose twelve of them, whom He also named as apostles. Simon, whom He also named Peter, and Andrew his brother; and James and John; and Philip and Bartholomew; and Matthew and Thomas; James the son of Alphaeus, and Simon who was called the Zealot; Judas the son of James, and Judas Iscariot, who became a traitor. And He descended with them, and stood on a level place; and there was a great multitude of His disciples and a great throng of people from all Judea and Jerusalem and the coastal region of Tyre and Sidon.*

2) Mark 3:14-15, 19 gives a little more information. *"And He appointed twelve, that they might be with Him, and that He might send them out to preach, and to have authority to cast out the demons: <u>and Judas Iscariot, who also betrayed Him</u>."*

3) Matthew 10:1, 4, 7-8—*"And having summoned His twelve disciples He gave them authority over unclean spirits, to cast them out, and to heal every kind of disease and every kind of sickness. Simon the Zealot, and Judas Iscariot the one who betrayed Him. And as you go, preach, saying, 'The kingdom of heaven is at hand. Heal the sick, raise the dead, cleanse the lepers, cast out demons; freely you received, freely give.'"*

Let's make our first list. Notice, it's quite impressive.

- after praying all night Jesus called His disciples (Luke 6:12-13)
- He chose the twelve, whom also He named apostles (Luke 6:13)
- and Judas Iscariot, who became a traitor (Luke 6:16)
- He appointed the twelve, that they might be with Him (Mark 3:14; Matt. 10:1)
- that He might send them out to preach (Mark 3:14; Matt. 10:7)
- He gave them authority to cast out the demons (Mark 3:15; Matt. 10:1)

- Judas Iscariot, who also betrayed him (Mark 3:19; Matt. 10:4)
- to heal all manner of disease and sickness (Matt. 10:1)
- raise the dead (Matt. 10:8)
- cleanse the lepers (Matt. 10:8)

Jesus spent all night praying before He chose the twelve. He named them apostles. These men were like ambassadors for Jesus. They were to preach that the kingdom of God was close at hand. To demonstrate that this was of God, Jesus gave them authority to cast out demons, heal the sick, and the ability to raise the dead. Keep in mind that this power comes from the Holy Spirit.

4) John 6:63-71—*It is the Spirit who gives life; the flesh profits nothing: the words that I have spoken to you are spirit, and are life. But there are some of you who do not believe. For Jesus knew from the beginning who they were who did not believe, and who it was that would betray Him. He was saying, "For this reason I have said to you, that no one can come to Me, unless it has been granted him from the Father." As a result of this many of His disciples withdrew, and were not walking with Him anymore. Jesus said therefore to the twelve, "You do not want to go away also, do you?" Simon Peter answered Him, "Lord, to whom shall we go? You have words of eternal life. And we have*

> *believed and have come to know that You are*
> *the Holy One of God." Jesus answered them,*
> *"Did I Myself not choose you, the twelve, and*
> <u>*yet one of you is a devil?" Now He meant*</u>
> <u>*Judas the son of Simon Iscariot, for he, one*</u>
> <u>*of the twelve, was going to betray Him*</u>.

Let's see what else we can learn:

- Judas did not believe in Jesus (John 6:64)
- Judas would betray Jesus (John 6:64)
- Jesus calls Judas a *devil* (John 6:70-71)

Jesus even knew at the time He picked Judas to be an apostle that he did not believe and would become a traitor. This really raises a lot of questions! Also look at this: ***And He was saying, <u>"For this reason***</u> ***<u>I have said to you, that no one can come to Me,</u>*** ***<u>unless it has been granted him from the Father." As</u>*** ***<u>a result of this many of His disciples withdrew, and</u>*** ***<u>were not walking with Him anymore</u>.*** Because many of Jesus' disciples really did not believe, He makes a powerful statement, ***<u>"That no one can come to Me,</u>*** ***<u>unless it has been granted him from the Father."</u>*** Jesus is saying that *no man* can become saved unless God grants it. This was too hard a word. It didn't feel good, and many of His disciples did not like it. So they walked away from Jesus, never to go back.

This year I've learned two things. One, I'm not in control. I thought I was, and you might think you are. The fact is that God's the only one in control. The second thing I've learned, and please don't miss this, is that I had created God in my image. You know, the kind of God that fits neatly into *my box*. We all do it. We wrap God up in all the Scriptures we like and it feels good and we say, "Here's my God." However, if we honestly approach the Scriptures, all of them, we find a God that we don't understand. He says a lot of hard words, and too many times we find Him doing things that a loving God would not do. This, of course, is from our puny little perspective.

When we have a real relationship with God, He spends our entire lives showing us who He *really* is. Then He asks, *"Will you serve me anyway?"* I believe the truly saved, no matter how long they wrestle with Him, will surrender and say, "Yes Lord!", even if it is with a broken heart. But for those who do not believe, they will *never* settle for who God really is.

Well, let's keep going.

5) John 12:3-8—*Mary therefore took a pound of very costly perfume of pure nard, and anointed the feet of Jesus, and wiped His feet with her hair; and the house was filled with the fragrance of the perfume. But <u>Judas Iscariot, one of His disciples, who was intending to betray Him</u>, said, "Why was this perfume not sold for three hundred denarii, and given to poor people?" <u>Now he said this, not because he was concerned about the poor, but because he was a thief, and as he had the money box, he used to pilfer what was put into it</u>. Jesus therefore said, "Let her alone, in order that she may keep it for the*

day of My burial. For the poor you always have with you, but you do not always have Me." See also Matthew 26:6-13 and Mark 14:1-9.

- Judas did not care about the poor (John 12:6).
- Judas was a thief (John 12:6).

In this Scripture, we have Judas Iscariot complaining about the apparent waste of this perfume, saying that it could be used for the poor. But what does the Bible tell us about his heart? *"Not because he was concerned about the poor, but because he was a thief, and as he had the money box, he used to pilfer what was put into it."* Judas had *no* concern for the poor. He just wanted more money to steal. So why would Jesus give him the moneybox? Strange, isn't it?

Following this event, Judas left and went to the chief priests, in order to betray Jesus. Read with me.

6) Mark 14: 10-11 — *"And Judas Iscariot, who was one of the twelve, went off to the chief priests, in order to betray Him [Jesus] to them. And they were glad when they heard this, and promised to give him money. And he began seeking how to betray Him at an opportune time."*

7) Luke 22:1-6 — *"Now the Feast of Unleavened Bread, which is called the Passover was approaching. And the chief priest and the*

scribes were seeking how they might put Him to death; for they were afraid of the people. And Satan entered into Judas who was called Iscariot, belonging to the number of the twelve. And he went away and discussed with the chief priests and officers how he might betray Him to them. And they were glad, and agreed to give him money. And he consented, and began seeking a good opportunity to betray Him to them apart from the multitude. " See also Matthew 26:14-16.

List:

- Judas went to the priests to discuss delivering Jesus to them (Mark 14:10).
- Judas was going to get money from the priests for betraying Jesus (Mark 14:11; Luke 22:4). Remember, he was a thief.
- Satan entered Judas (Luke 22:3).
- Judas sought for the right opportunity to betray Jesus (Luke 22:6).

So far the Bible does not hint at anything that might cause us to think that Judas Iscariot was a true believer. In fact, it has exposed his heart as being wicked. Go with me now to the Last Supper.

8) Matthew 26:20-25—*Now when evening had come, He was reclining the table with the twelve disciples. And as they were eating, He said, "Truly I say to you that one of you will*

betray Me." *And being deeply grieved, they each one began to say to Him, "Surely not I, Lord?" And He answered and said, "He who dipped his hand with Me in the bowl is the one who will betray Me. The Son of Man is to go, just as it is written of Him; but woe to that man by whom the Son of Man is betrayed! It would have been good for that man if he had not been born." And Judas, who was betraying Him, answered and said, "Surely it is not I, Rabbi?" He said to him, "You have said it yourself."*

9) John 13:1-2; 26-30—*Now before the Feast of the Passover, Jesus knowing that His hour had come that He should depart out of this world to the Father, having loved His own who were in the world, He loved them to the end. And during supper, the devil having already put into the heart of Judas Iscariot, the son of Simon, to betray Him, Jesus therefore answered, "That is the one for whom I shall dip the morsel and give it to him." So when He had dipped the morsel, He took and gave it to Judas, the son Simon Iscariot." And after the morsel Satan then entered into him. Jesus therefore said to him, "What you do, do quickly." Now no one of those reclining at the table knew for what purpose He had said this to him. For some were supposing, because Judas had the money box, that Jesus was saying to*

him, "Buy the things we have need of for the feast"; or else, that he should give something to the poor. And so after receiving the morsel he went out immediately; and it was night. See also Luke 22:21-23 and Mark 14:17-21.

List:

- Jesus said, "One of you will betray me" (Matt. 26:21).
- Jesus said, "He who dipped his hand with Me in the bowl is the one who will betray me" (Matt. 26:23; John 13:26).
- "Woe to that man by whom the Son of man is betrayed! It would have been good for that man if he had not been born" (Matt. 26:24).
- Judas who betrayed him, answered and said, "Surely it is not I Rabbi?" He said to him, "You have said it yourself" (Matt. 26:25).
- The devil having already put into the heart of Judas Iscariot, the son of Simon, to betray him (John 13:2).
- And after the morsel, Satan entered into him (John 13:27).
- Judas having received the morsel went out immediately; and it was night (John 13:30).

Let's talk about some of these things. The Bible is clear that this man, Judas Iscariot, the son of Simon, is the one who betrayed Jesus. But what is amazing to me, is when Jesus told His disciples that one of them would betray Him, nobody accused Judas. He fit in so well with the other apostles. No one suspected him as a traitor. But that's what traitors do!

I want us to also take notice of the other apostles' response when Jesus said that one of them would betray Him. *"And being deeply grieved, they each one began to say to Him, 'Surely not I, Lord?'"* This truly breaks my heart, because I know that some of you who are truly one of God's own children will ask the same question. The struggle can be overwhelming. Please know I grieve with you, and I'm sorry that these truths might bring you pain. I ask that as you wrestle with God for your answers that you will count your suffering worth it, if those who are deceived might truly find Jesus!

In Matthew 26:24, Jesus said that it was better for Judas *not* to have been born. Now the only thing I can think of worse than not being born is to die and go to hell. Jesus opens that verse with a, woe. Trust me, Jesus saying woe to anybody is not a good thing. Next we see that Judas has been possessed by Satan, again. We need to ask: Can a believer become possessed by the devil? According to Scripture I don't think it's possible. You should search and find that out for yourself. We also find that Satan put in Judas' heart to betray Jesus. It's clear to see who is running Judas' life—it's not God!

Still nothing that would lead us to believe that this man was a true follower of Jesus, except that Jesus choose him to be an apostle, and he was given the same power and authority as the other eleven.

I would like to bring something to your attention. *"And so after receiving the morsel he went out immediately; and it was night" (John 13:30).* From this point until we find Judas betraying Jesus in the garden, Judas was not with Jesus or the other eleven. So everything that Jesus said to His other apostles, the rest of John 13 through chapter 17, and along with the other gospels, was spoken just to these men. That is interesting when you read what Jesus said.

Now I would like us to go back to John 13 and see what else it might tell us about Judas:

10) John 13:3-18—*Jesus, knowing that the Father had given all the things into His hands, and that He come forth from God, and was going back to God, rose from supper, and laid aside His garments; and taking a towel, He girded himself about. Then He poured water into the basin, and began to wash the disciples' feet, and to wipe them with the towel with which He was girded. So He came to Simon Peter. He said to Him, "Lord, do you wash my feet?" Jesus answered and said unto him, "What I do you do not realize now, but you shall understand hereafter." Peter said to Him, "Never shall you wash my feet!" Jesus answered him, "If I do not wash you, you have no part with Me." Simon Peter said to Him, "Lord, not my feet only, but also my hands and my head." Jesus said to him, "He who has bathed needs only to wash his feet, but is completely clean; and you are clean, but not all of you." For He knew*

the one who was betraying Him; for this reason He said, "Not all of you are clean." And so when He had washed their feet, and taken His garments, and reclined at the table again, He said to them, "Do you know what I have done to you? You call Me Teacher, and Lord; and you are right, for so I am. If I then, the Lord and the Teacher, washed your feet, you also ought to wash one another's feet. For I gave you an example, that you also should do as I did to you. Truly, truly, I say to you, a slave is not greater than his master; neither is one who is sent greater than the one who sent him. If you know these things, you are blessed if you do them. I do not speak of all of you. I know the ones I have chosen; but it is that the Scripture may be fulfilled, "He who eats My bread has lifted up his heel against Me."

List:

- Jesus said that Judas was *not* clean like the rest of the apostles (John 13:10-11).
- Jesus said, *"If you know these things, you are blessed if you do them. I do speak not of all of you"* (John 13:17-18).
- Jesus said, *"I know whom I have chosen; but that the Scripture may be fulfilled, 'He who eats My bread has lifted up his heel against Me'"* (John 13:18).

Jesus is telling us something very significant about Judas. He's not clean! Jesus is exposing the condition of Judas' heart, and it's evil. Jesus also makes it clear in verse 18 that all that He just mentioned, about how the apostles needed to serve each other, and that they would be blessed if they did this, did not apply to Judas!

Remember in our first list, how Jesus choose the twelve apostles? Here He tells us why He choose Judas, "But it is that the Scripture may be fulfilled, *"He who eats My bread has lifted up his heel against Me."* This is quoted from Psalm 41:9, *"Even My close friend, in whom I trusted, who ate my bread, has lifted up his heel against me."* Jesus never did away with the Law or the prophets, He fulfilled them.

Next we'll turn to Jesus praying to His heavenly Father for all those that God had given Him. Let's read.

11) John 17:10-12—

> *And all things that are Mine are Thine, and Thine are Mine; and I have been glorified in them. And I am no more in the world; and yet they themselves are in the world, and I come to Thee. Holy Father, keep them in Thy name, the name which Thou hast given Me, that they may be one, even as We are. While I was with them, I was keeping them in Thy name which Thou hast given Me; and I guarded them, <u>and not one of them</u>*

perished but the SON OF PERDITION, that the Scripture might be fulfilled.

In verse 12 Jesus said, *"Not one of them perished."* He lets us know that He does *not* lose any of those entrusted to Him. When we are *in* Christ we do have eternal life. Praise God! Next, Jesus said, *"But the SON OF PERDITION, that the Scripture might be fulfilled."* The only one that would perish was the one that was not His to start with. The reason Jesus chose Judas was that the Scripture might be fulfilled. Now look at the phrase, *"son of perdition."* This is only used here and one other time in the New Testament (2 Thessalonians 2:1-4). Let's read it:

12) 2 Thessalonians 2:1-4—

> *Now we request you, brethren, with regard to the coming of our Lord Jesus Christ, and our gathering together to Him, that you may not be quickly shaken from your composure or be disturbed either by a spirit or a message or a letter as if from us, to the effect that the day of the Lord has come. Let no one in any way deceive you, for it will not come unless the apostasy comes first, and the man of lawlessness is revealed, THE SON OF DESTRUCTION, who opposes and exalts himself above every so-called god or object of worship, so that he takes his seat in the temple of God, displaying himself as being God."*

In these two Scriptures, *"the son of perdition"* and *"the son of destruction"* are the same words. Perdition/destruction means ruin or loss, spiritual and eternal. This hints, to the destiny of the person mentioned in John; namely, Judas. It gives a suggestion to the antichrist in Thessalonians, referring to one determined to remain spiritually lost.

In John 17:12, Jesus said that, *"**not one of them perished but [Judas] the son of perdition.**"* The word *perished* means the same here as it does in John 3:16-18—eternally lost without God. *"**For God so loved the world, that He gave His only begotten Son, that whoever believes in Him should not** perish**, but have eternal life. For God did not send the Son into the world to judge the world, but that the world should be saved through Him. He who believes in Him is not judged; he who does not believe has been judged already, because he has not believed in the name of the only begotten Son of God.**"*

We are about halfway finished with this chapter. I know we've covered a lot, but it was needful.

13) Matthew 27:1-6—

> *Now when morning had come, all the chief priests and the elders of the people took counsel against Jesus to put Him to death; and they bound Him, and led Him away, and delivered Him up to Pilate the governor. Then **when Judas, who had betrayed Him, saw that He had been condemned, he felt***

> *remorse and returned the thirty pieces of*
> *silver to the chief priests and elders, saying,*
> *"I have sinned by betraying innocent blood."*
> *But they said, "What is that to us? See to*
> *that yourself!" And he threw the pieces of*
> *silver into the sanctuary and departed; and*
> *he went away and hanged himself. And the*
> *chief priests took the pieces of silver and said,*
> *"It is not lawful to put them into the temple*
> *treasury, since it is the price of blood."*

List:

- When Judas saw Jesus was condemned, *he felt remorse* (Matt. 27:3).
- *He returned the thirty pieces of silver* to the chief priests and elders (Matt. 27:3).
- Judas said, "*I have sinned by betraying innocent blood*" (Matt. 27:4).
- He threw the money into the sanctuary (Matt. 27:5).
- He left, went away, and *hanged himself* (Matt. 27:5).

The Scripture says Judas felt *remorse* (some translations use the word repent), confessed his sin, went away, and hung himself. This is the *only* Scripture that could give us hope that Judas made things right at the end. So let's take a look at the definitions of some of these words. First, *remorse* is not the same word as *repent*, that John the Baptist and Jesus used in Matthew 3:1-2: *"Now in those days John the*

***Baptist came, preaching in the wilderness of Judea,
saying, "Repent, for the kingdom of heaven is at
hand."*** And Matthew 4:17: ***"From that time Jesus
began to preach and say, 'Repent, for the kingdom
of heaven is at hand.'"*** The word, *repent* that Jesus
and John used means to regret what you have done;
it is always followed by a true change of heart toward
God.

Judas felt remorse. Indeed, he regretted that he
had betrayed Jesus. He wished he could have changed
what he did. Nevertheless, this remorse did not
produce a change of heart, or salvation. We can see
that a person can have worldly sorrow, weep, and cry,
yet true repentance not take place. There is a difference between conscience and conviction. All men at
some time or another have felt remorse for certain
things they've done. However, true conviction brings
about a change in a man. Judas had rejected Christ
and killed himself.

Judas could have received forgiveness if he
wanted to. Even in this, he chose to take care of
his sin himself. I believe this is the worst tragedy
possible—to come this close to Jesus and fall away.
I had a friend named Brother Norman, who once
said, "Men can come all the way to the cross and still
not get under the blood." This is Judas. He is called
the son of perdition just like the antichrist. He was a
thief; Jesus called him a devil, and Satan entered him.
Although Judas was sorry for what he did, it was not
the repenting of the heart that causes the saving of
one's soul.

14) Acts 1:15-20—

And at this time Peter stood up in the midst of the brethren (a gathering of about one hundred and twenty persons was there together), and said, "<u>Brethren, the Scripture had to be fulfilled, which the Holy Spirit foretold by the mouth of David concerning Judas, who became a guide to those who arrested Jesus. For he was counted among us, and received his portion in this ministry.</u>" (Now this man acquired a field with the <u>price of his wickedness</u>; and falling headlong, he burst open in the middle and all his bowels gushed out. And it became known to all who were living in Jerusalem; so that in their own language that field was called Hakeldama, that is, Field of Blood. For it is written in the book of Psalms, "Let his homestead be made desolate, and let no man dwell in it; and, his office let another man take."

List:

- He became a guide to those who arrested Jesus (Acts 1:16).
- *Judas was counted among the apostles* (Acts 1:17).
- He *received his portion in that ministry* (Acts 1:17).
- He acquired a field with the price of *his wickedness* (Acts 1:18).

- Judas, falling headlong, burst open in the middle and all his bowels gushed out (Acts 1:18).
- That field was called Hakeldama, that is, Field of Blood (Acts 1:19).
- Let his homestead be made desolate, and let no man dwell in it; and, his office let another man take" (Acts 1:20).

Look at the words used in this last passage about Judas—wickedness, bowels gushing out, Field of Blood, desolate. Not words that are connected to true believers. Yet in this passage, verse 17 says, *"For he was counted among us, and received his portion in this ministry."* This is very interesting and reminds me of some tough Scripture found in Hebrews 6.

Turn with me and let's read Hebrews 6:1-9:

Therefore leaving the elementary teaching about the Christ, let us press on to maturity, not laying again a foundation of repentance from dead works and of faith toward God, of instruction about washings, and laying on of hands, and the resurrection of the dead, and eternal judgment. And this we shall do, if God permits. For in the case of those who have once been enlightened and have tasted of the heavenly gift and have been made partakers of the Holy Spirit, and have tasted the good word of God and the powers of the age to come, and then have fallen away, it is impossible to renew them again to repen-

tance, since they again crucify to themselves the Son of God, and put Him to open shame. For ground that drinks the rain which often falls upon it and brings forth vegetation useful to those for whose sake it is also tilled, receives a blessing from God; but if it yields thorns and thistles, it is worthless and close to being cursed, and it ends up being burned. But, beloved, we are convinced of better things concerning you, and things that accompany salvation, though we are speaking in this way.

This is a difficult passage and for ages scholars have disagreed about its meaning. I see two possible interpretations to this Scripture:

1) A person can be truly born again and fall away. In another words, that they can lose their salvation.

2) A person can experience all the things mentioned and be lost, revealing that they were never truly born again to start with.

I believe that these verses are referring to a person who came so close to Jesus and His truths, yet ended up rejecting Him. I believe that Judas fits the descriptions given in Hebrews 6. He was one of the chosen apostles. He was given great spiritual gifts, authority, and the ability to preach the kingdom of heaven. Yet we see that he rejected Jesus and perished.

Let's make our list, starting at verse four: ,

- Those who have once been *enlightened*
- have *tasted* of the heavenly gift
- have been made *partakers* of the Holy spirit
- have *tasted* the good Word of God
- have *tasted* the powers of the world to come
- and *then* have *fallen away.*
- It's *impossible* to *renew them again to repentance*
- since *they* again *crucify* to themselves *the Son of God and put Him to open shame.*

Before we look at the definitions, we need to understand that translating from one language written two thousand years ago to ours today is not easy. Many times the Greek word might make a whole phrase in the English language.

Like this phrase: "those who were once enlightened." It's made up of two Greek words, the first of which means to make one see or understand. The second word means briefly or quickly. This person had been *enlightened* by the gospel. But man is not saved just because he has become enlightened to spiritual truths. In John 1:1-9, we see the word enlightened also used.

In the beginning was the Word, and the Word was with God, and the Word was God. He was in the beginning with God. All things came into being by Him, and apart from Him nothing came into being that has come into being. In Him was life, and the life was the light of men. And <u>the light</u>

*shines in the darkness, and the darkness did
not comprehend it. There came a man, sent
from God, whose name was John. He came
for a witness, that he might bear witness
of the light, that all might believe through
him. He was not the light, but came that he
might bear witness of the light. There was
the true light which, coming into the world,
ENLIGHTENS every man."*

Verse nine says that Jesus enlightens every man.

Next, the word *tasted*. Basically, it means *to
experience something*. Please keep in mind that there
is a difference between tasting and consuming. In
this Scripture it says that these people tasted three
things:

1) The heavenly gift—I'm not sure what this
   is. It's not real clear, but I believe it could be
   grace, God's unmerited favor. Does God give
   His grace to all men? I believe to some degree,
   yes. *God causes the sun to rise on the evil
   and the good, and sends rain on the righteous and the unrighteous,* Matt. 5:43-45.
2) They tasted the Word of God—These people
   experienced God's truths. Many people have
   been blessed by God's Word; the lost and the
   saved.
3) The powers of the world to come—The word
   for power here means to have achieving
   power. Remember what Judas was given by
   Jesus to do? The power and authority to cast

out demons, heal the sick, raise the dead, and preach effectively.

Sounds just like Matthew 7:21-23: *"Not everyone who says to Me [Jesus] 'Lord, Lord' will enter the kingdom of heaven; but he who DOES the will of My Father who is in heaven. Many will say to Me on that day, 'Lord, Lord, did we not prophesy in Your name, and in Your name cast out demons, and in Your name perform many miracles?' And then I will declare to them, 'I NEVER KNEW YOU; depart from Me, you who practice lawlessness.'"* Although Judas did all the things mentioned above, we are reminded that he was a thief and full of wickedness.

"And have been made partakers of the Holy Spirit." This phrase could be puzzling for most people. This is because we've been taught that the *only* people moved by the Holy Spirit are true Christians. That's just not so. First, we know that the gifts Judas flowed in were given to him by Jesus. We also know that the working *out* of the gifts is through the Holy Spirit.

Actually, we find many examples in the Bible where God moved lost men by the Holy Spirit to accomplish His work. For one, Balaam; he was a false prophet, who the Spirit of the Lord came upon to bless Israel (Numbers 24:2). You'll find the whole story in Numbers 22–24. When you read it, make a list of how the Scripture describes Balaam. There are many more if you will search them out.

Let's look at Hebrews 6:6: *"And then have fallen away, it is impossible to renew them again to repentance, since they again crucify to themselves the Son of God, and put Him to open shame."*

These people just walked away from Jesus. They rejected the only sacrifice for their sins so it is impossible to have true repentance. Just because people believe truth, does not mean that they embrace it. You can know the truth yet chose not to obey it. This is what Judas did.

Remember in the sower and the seed from Mark 4:16-19—

And in a similar way these are the ones on whom seed was sown on the rocky places, who, when they hear the word, immediately receive it with joy; and they have no firm root in themselves, but are only temporary; then, when affliction or persecution arises because of the word, immediately they fall away. And others are the ones on whom seed was sown among the thorns; these are the ones who have heard the word, and the worries of the world, and the deceitfulness of riches, and the desires for other things enter in and choke the word, and it becomes unfruitful.

Either of these two soils could describe Judas. He believed for a while, and then rejected Jesus. The gospel was choked and no salvation was produced.

"For if we go on sinning willfully after receiving the knowledge of the truth, there no longer remains a sacrifice for sins, but a certain terrifying expecta-

tion of judgment, and the fury of a fire which will consume the adversaries"

I believe Judas fits all the qualifications in Hebrews 6:4-6. Therefore, we can conclude that a person can talk and look so much like a Christian, even do mighty works, and yet be "but almost a Christian."

Let me close with an excerpt from Mr. Mead's book.

> Know this, that natural conscience is capable of great improvements from the means of grace. Sitting under the ordinances may exceedingly heighten the endowments of conscience. It may be much regulated though it is not at all renewed. It may be enlightened and convinced, yet never savingly converted and changed. You read in Hebrews 6:4 of some who were enlightened, tasted of the heavenly gift, and were made partakers of the Holy Ghost. What work shall we call this? It could not be a saving work, a true change and conversion of state for, notwithstanding this enlightening, tasting, and partaking, they are said to fall away, verse 6. Had it been a true grace, they could never have fallen away from that. A believer may fall but he cannot fall away. He may fall foully but he cannot fall finally, for underneath are the everlasting arms. His faith is established in the strength of that prayer of Christ that our faith fail not. Nay, He tells us expressly that it is eternal life

which He gives from which we shall never perish.

List of Judas

- After praying all night Jesus called His disciples (Luke 6:12-13).
- He chose the twelve, whom also He named apostles (Luke 6:13)
- and Judas Iscariot, who became a traitor (Luke 6:16).
- He appointed the twelve, that they might be with Him (Mark 3:14; Matt. 10:1)
- that He might send them out to preach (Mark 3:14; Matt. 10:7).
- He gave them authority to cast out the demons (Mark 3:15; Matt. 10:1).
- Judas Iscariot, who also betrayed him (Mark 3:19; Matt. 10:4).
- To heal all manner of disease and sickness (Matt. 10:1)
- raise the dead (Matt. 10:8)
- cleanse the lepers (Matt. 10:8).
- He did not believe in Jesus (John 6:64).
- He would betray Jesus (John 6:64).
- Jesus calls him *a devil* (John 6:70-71).
- Judas did not care about the poor (John 12:6).
- Judas was a thief (John 12:6).
- Judas went to the priests to discuss delivering Jesus to them (Mark 14:10).

- Judas was going to get money from the priests for betraying Jesus (Mark 14:11; Luke 22:4). Remember, he was a thief.
- Satan entered Judas (Luke 22:3).
- Judas sought for the right opportunity to betray Jesus (Luke 22:6).
- Jesus said, "That one of you will betray me" (Matt. 26:21).
- Jesus said, "He who dipped his hand with Me in the bowl is the one who will betray Me" (Matt. 26:23; John 13:26).
- "Woe to that man by whom the Son of man is betrayed! It would have been good for that man if he had not been born" (Matt. 26:24).
- Judas answered and said, "Surely it is not I Rabbi?" He said to him, "You have said it yourself" (Matt. 26:25).
- The devil having already put into the heart of Judas Iscariot, the son of Simon, to betray him" (John 13:2).
- And after the morsel, Satan entered into him (John 13:27).
- Judas, having received the morsel, went out immediately; and it was night (John 13:30).
- Jesus said that Judas was *not* clean like the rest of the disciples (John 13:10-11).
- Jesus said, ***"If you know these things, you are blessed if you do them."*** Jesus is *not* talking about Judas (John 13:17-18).
- Jesus choose Judas as one of the twelve, just to fulfill Scripture (John 13:18; Psalm 41:9;

"He who eats My bread has lifted up his heel against Me."

- Jesus called Judas the son of perdition (or son of destruction) and he is lost (John 17:12). This refers to the antichrist (2 Thess. 2:1-4).
- When Judas saw that Jesus was condemned, *he felt remorse* (Matt. 27:3).
- He returned the thirty pieces of silver to the chief priests and elders (Matt. 27:3).
- Judas said, *"I have sinned by betraying innocent blood"* (Matt. 27:4).
- He threw the money into the sanctuary (Matt. 27:5).
- He left, went away, and *hanged himself* (Matt. 27:5).
- He became a guide to those who arrested Jesus (Acts 1:16).
- *Judas was counted among the apostles* (Acts 1:17).
- He *received his portion of that ministry* (Acts 1:17).
- He acquired a field with the price of *his wickedness* (Acts 1:18).

Conclusion

✣

As I close this book, I feel that many of you are asking about grace. I hear people always say, "Yes, but we are no longer *under* the law. We are *under grace*." To that I say a hearty AMEN! But if you tell me that this means God overlooks our sin, I will have to disagree. I know that Christians can and do sin. I do! However, if you are using that as an excuse to sin, and you're not grieved deeply when you do, then I would be concerned.

Unfortunately, many who quote that have no idea where it is in the Bible, nor do they know the full passage. Read with me, Romans 6:14-15—*"For sin SHALL NOT be master over you, for you are not under law, but under grace. What then? Shall we sin because we are not under law but under grace? May it never be!"* It's clear from Paul's statements here and the whole chapter that grace really means, when you are born again, and under grace, sin is no longer your master. Romans 6:17-18—*"But thanks be to God that though you WERE slaves of sin, you became obedient from the heart to that form of teaching to which you were committed, and having been freed from sin, you became slaves of righteousness."* When we are under grace we are slaves of righteousness, which means we will begin to live that way.

It all boils down to the heart. If we are truly struggling with sin, we, like Paul, will say, *"Wretched man that I am! Who will set me free from the body of this death?"* Then we'll run to Christ for our deliverance and forgiveness. *"Thanks be to God through Jesus Christ our Lord!"* Yes, then God's grace is available. He forgives and continues to help us overcome. Regrettably, a lot of people think that God's grace (His unmerited favor), means that you can sin all you want and it is OK now that you are a "believer"! *Never!* It's not possible.

Because it is written, "You shall be holy, for I am holy" (1 Peter 1:16).

It's unnerving; some of the questions people ask me on this subject. Many times people are interested in how much sin they can have in their lives and still make heaven. Or, how long can they walk away from Jesus and still be considered saved. I do not have those answers. What I do know is that the church for too long has preached a one-sided message. We've shouted, "Grace, Grace!" and that is true. Nevertheless, we must consider the whole counsel of God. The Scriptures we've covered in this book must be reckoned with.

"For from the least of them even to the greatest of them, everyone is greedy for gain, and from the prophet even to the priest everyone deals falsely. And they have healed the brokenness of My people superficially, saying, 'Peace, peace' but there is no peace!" (Jeremiah 6:13-14).

I believe if we truly belong to God, our heart's cry would be, "Is there enough room for me also to lean on Jesus?" What about YOU!

Bibliography

New American Standard Bible. La Habra, CA: The Lockman Foundation, 1960, 1962, 1968, 1971, 1972, 1973, 1974, 1977. Used with permission.

Mead, Matthew. *The Almost Christian Discovered.* Pennsylvania: Soli Deo Gloria Publications, 1993. Used with permission.

Murray Andrew. *The Blood of Christ.* Michigan: Bethany House Publishers, 2001.

Printed in the United States
214508BV00001B/3/P